Catch Fire

A Call for Revival

Brenton MacArthur Barnett

Copyrights and Permissions

Unless otherwise indicated, Scripture quotations are taken from the New American Standard Bible®, Copyright © 1960, 1962, 1963, 1968, 1971, 1972, 1973, 1975, 1977, 1995 by The Lockman Foundation. Used by permission. (www.Lockman.org)

Copyright © 2020, Brenton MacArthur Barnett
First Edition

Without limiting the rights under copyright reserved above,
no part of this publication may be reproduced,
stored in or introduced into a retrieval system,
or transmitted, in any form or by any means
(electronic, mechanical, photocopying, recording, or otherwise),
without the prior written permission of both the copyright owner
and the publisher of this book.

Published by Aventine Press
55 E Emerson St.
Chula Vista CA 91911
www.aventinepress.com

ISBN: 978-1-59330-976-3

Printed in the United States of America

ALL RIGHTS RESERVED

Dedication

To the Lord, for His grace to bear with me as I continue to press on in human weakness to more adequately understand His infallible and inalterable truth

To my precious and beautiful wife, Sarah, whose constant and steadfast love for me encourages me and strengthens me to continue to strive to be the best husband, father, and man that I can be

Table of Contents

Introduction: Re-examining Revival 7

Section 1: If My People Will Humble Themselves

    Chapter 1: What Really Is Humility? 17
    Chapter 2: Cease Operating on Human Strength
                and Ingenuity 23
    Chapter 3: Surrender Absolutely to God's Authority 37

Section 2: If My People Will Pray...

    Chapter 4: What Is God's Design for Prayer? 51
    Chapter 5: Commit to Corporate and Individual Prayer 61

Section 3: If My People Will Seek My Face...

    Chapter 6: What Does It Mean to Seek God's Face? 77
    Chapter 7: Develop a Mature Biblical Framework
                of Knowledge 83

Section 4: If My People Will Turn from Their Wicked Ways...

    Chapter 8: What Is True Repentance? 95
    Chapter 9: Return to a Lifestyle of Personal Holiness 101
    Chapter 10: Cultivate Corporate Holiness 111
    Chapter 11: Evangelize Biblically 121

Section 5: Then I Will Hear, Forgive, and Heal Their Land

    Chapter 12: The Beautiful Bride 135

Introduction: Re-examining Revival

Before digging into the specifics ailing our modern churches, we need to understand the Biblical definition of revival and how God sends revival. The principles are really straightforward, but the church by and large rejects God's fundamental truths. As we study the Scripture's teaching on revival, we ought to be challenged concerning sin in our lives, convicted as to our callous view of the Bible, and encouraged to spread the truth of the uncompromised gospel before time runs out.

What Is Revival?

There is a great deal of misunderstanding about revival. For some, revival is a historic moving of God where many people confess sins and turn to Christ for the first time. For others, revival is a tent meeting where people are invited and the gospel is preached. For others still, revival is something marked by emotional outburst and supernatural manifestations. The best way to sort out the fact from the fiction is to look at how God's Word speaks of revival and to consider some actual Biblical examples. This is the only way to understand revival objectively and in terms of absolutes. Without Scripture, we are left to mere subjectivity and opinion, getting us nowhere fast.

First, we should consider the etymology of the word "revival" itself. It is derived from the Latin word *revivere*. The "re" prefix means "again," and the "vivere" portion means "to live." So if we put the two parts together, we get *revive* which means, by conclusion, "to live again."

Next, we should consider the literal meaning of the word which is "to start again." Synonyms include the following: arouse, awaken, bounce back, brighten, bring to, cheer, encourage, energize, enkindle, enliven, exhilarate, gladden, invigorate, make whole, overcome, rally, recondition, recover, refresh, rejuvenate, resuscitate, renovate, restore, revitalize, rouse, strengthen, touch up, and wake up. There is an overarching theme of taking something or someone that was once vibrant and alive and bringing it or them back to full energy and intensity.

Finally, we should look at some uses of the word "revived" in the Scriptures. Using Scripture to interpret Scripture is a very important and helpful tool. 2 Kings 13:21 says, "As they were burying a man, behold, they saw a marauding band; and they cast the man into the grave of Elisha. And when the man touched the bones of Elisha he revived and stood up on his feet." 1 Kings 17:22 says, "The LORD heard the voice of Elijah, and the life of the child returned to him and he revived." 1 Samuel 30:11-13 says, "Now they found an Egyptian in the field and brought him to David, and gave him bread and he ate, and they provided him water to drink. They gave him a piece of fig cake and two clusters of raisins, and he ate; then his spirit revived. For he had not eaten bread or drunk water for three days and three nights." Lastly, Genesis 45:26-27 says, "They told him, saying, 'Joseph is still alive, and indeed he is ruler over all the land of Egypt.' But he was stunned, for he did not believe them. When they told him all the words of Joseph that he had spoken to them, and when he saw the wagons that Joseph had sent to carry him, the spirit of their father Jacob revived." In these passages we see instances of individuals who were physically alive, who then died, and who were then resurrected. We also see a person who was famished physically who then revived upon eating food and drinking water. We then see Jacob who was spiritually and emotionally drained until he saw the wagons and realized that Joseph was alive. Then His spirit revived. These uses of the word "revived" are, of course, physical in nature, but the principle can translate to the spiritual. The idea is that in order to be revived physically, one has to first be alive or vibrant. Something then happens to sap that life and strength. Finally, when people are revived, their life and strength return. The spiritual truth is that only those who have first been made alive can truly be revived in the technical sense. In other words, revival is for believers because they have already been made alive in Christ. Something happened as their hearts were entangled by the deceitfulness of sin such that their walks with Christ were severely weakened. In order to get them back to the same spiritual health that they once had, they need revival. They need to get back to what had made them strong in the Lord in the first place. If revival is to occur, those who truly know Christ need to be first reawakened to the truth of the Scriptures and to obedience to Christ. Then, their lives will lead to effective evangelistic impact of the world.

Of course, God may reach out to somebody who doesn't know Him and work to lead them to the gospel. But this is not the main way that God works, for He has called us as messengers of good news with a call to preach and teach the gospel (Acts 1:8). The more alive and pure the church is, the more clearly the world will be able to see Jesus and the more sense the gospel will make.

So, first and foremost, revival clearly speaks to God's work within the believer. Psalm 119:93 says, "I will never forget your precepts, for by them you have revived me." In verse 37 he says, "Turn my eyes from looking at vanity, And revive me in Your ways." In verse 88 he continues, "Revive me according to Your lovingkindness, So that I may keep the testimony of Your mouth." And in verse 107, he says, "I am exceedingly afflicted; Revive me according to Your Word." As the Psalmist encountered various life events and struggles, he called to God to revive his spirit. Afflictions, trials, and difficult circumstances can sap our faith and excitement for God as they wear us down. Falling into sin and indulging vanity will eliminate spiritual vitality. Wherever we might presently be at in our walks before the Lord, God's Word has something to say to us and a work of revival to generate within us. As God's Word is taught to our hearts by the Holy Spirit indwelling us, we can be revived. Apart from the truth of God's commands, we have no hope of revival. Apart from the Holy Spirit in our hearts, we have no hope of personal holiness. But as children of God indwelt by God and given His inalterable Word, revival is most certainly possible. And it starts with each of us individually before God.

Too often we think that we have to wait for some external stimulus, supernatural event, or church gathering in order for revival to break out. But the reality is that it happens person by person within the heart as the Holy Spirit convicts of sin and righteousness. When God's Word is read and preached in the public forum, many hearts can be touched at once, and there is no telling just how far-reaching the effects could be. This is why we can never neglect or underestimate the potency and necessity of reading and preaching God's sufficient, living, and active Word. In Nehemiah 8, the people of Israel gathered at the public square in Jerusalem and asked Ezra the scribe to read the book of the law to them. This went on for hours because the people's appetite for the Word and for revival was true. This was really a remarkable event. In fact, it is difficult to even picture this happening in our time and in our churches. Can you picture a group of believers pressuring the pastor to open the book of Romans and to begin reading it publicly verse by verse from sunrise to noon? Can you imagine being out with a bunch of friends and spontaneously deciding to read through Deuteronomy? Frankly, if a brother or sister in the Lord did make such a request to read God's Word at length, there would likely be honest groans and complaints as people would make excuses to leave. Revival doesn't stem from entertainment and the tickling of the ears but from truly meditating upon the righteous principles and attributes of God. Only when we are conformed to righteousness and seeking to keep moving in that direction can God begin a great work through His people.

In Nehemiah's time, the Israelites had a tremendous thirst for God. After they read the law, they began to weep. They confessed their sins and their fathers' sins. After hearing God's Word read for hours, they stood confessing and worshipping for another three hours. In chapter 10, they resolved to correct the areas in their lives which were not honoring to God, even signing a covenantal agreement between them and God. A genuine revival among God's people happened in Israel at that time, leading them to repentance, the culmination of any true revival. A similar occurrence happened when King Josiah found the law of God which had been misplaced and essentially lost as if nobody had their Bible anymore. The Bible became irrelevant for the chosen nation of God, but when Josiah found it, he read it and started to put its commands into practice. **This doesn't just lead to revival, but it is revival.** Revival starts as we open up God's Word and actually believe it and obey it. Revival is not rocket science or something that only a theology professor can understand. It is simple, and it is for those who are humble. **If we want to see revival, the preaching and reading of the Word in fullness and integrity must be a fundamental catalyst.**

Revival Reaches to the Unsaved

The wonderful thing about revived Christians is that they impact the world. They are noticed, for their testimony is legitimized. God gave Solomon wisdom and blessing, and dignitaries the world over such as the Queen of Sheba came to visit. They marveled at Solomon's wisdom, and the Queen of Sheba even acknowledged and worshipped God. The queen's conclusion in 2 Chronicles 9:8 was, "Blessed be the LORD your God who delighted in you, setting you on His throne as king for the LORD your God; because your God loved Israel establishing them forever, therefore He made you king over them, to do justice and righteousness." A foreign, pagan woman worshiped and blessed Jehovah, for she saw how God had a people excited about Him and committed to His ways. Such a people she realized could only be a blessing, and she was drawn to their God.

The overarching Scriptural design is for believers to catch fire and then transmit that excitement to reaching the lost, their lives even drawing the unsaved to Christ. Hebrews 12:14 says, "Pursue peace with all men and holiness, without which no one will see the Lord." It is our lives of holiness before the lost that compel and propel them to seek the things of God as the Spirit moves in their hearts. If we live as hypocrites, we do a great harm because we blind people from being able to see God. In John 13:34-35, Jesus said that the world can and should recognize us by our selfless Christlike love. In John 17:21, He took the principle a step further by praying "that they may be one, as I and the Father are One, so that the world may know that the Father sent the Son." A unified family, church family, or group of friends can do a great deal to encourage someone to put his or her faith in Christ. Of course, this is not just a unity based upon common interests but rather one that is founded upon having a common belief and a unified confession. The world recognizes us by our love and by our unity. They then watch these who profess to love God and see if they can get along with one another, a task that the world really struggles with given that sin is reigning in their bodies. If we are unified, then the Scripture says that the world will believe that Jesus really is God and that He did indeed come to earth. They are basically ready to receive the gospel. Unfortunately, if we are not loving, unified, or living holy lives, we are not helping anybody to see Christ. We bear a responsibility for not giving the Spirit opportunity to move, and we grieve Him. Matthew 5:16 says, "Let your light so shine before men that they may see your good works and glorify your Father who is in heaven." Like the Queen of Sheba blessing and glorifying God because of His work through the good deeds of men, so we too can help the lost glorify God by our selfless acts of love. All of these verses demonstrate that a revived Christian will begin to impact society and the lost. **This sets up the general rule that the lost get saved after the Christian is first revived.** This is not an absolute rule, for God works how He chooses. But generally it does seem to be a principle presented thematically throughout the Scriptures.

A revived person will naturally have opportunities to share his faith within his circles of influence. For example, a person at work might begin to ask questions or persecute, opening a door for conversation and interaction. It is possible to watch a person be convicted of sin before our very eyes simply because of how we live our lives for Christ. Such opportunities are open doors for the gospel. People will wonder why we have so much hope despite difficulty in our lives. That is an open door for us to give an answer concerning the gospel. As 1 Peter 3:15 says, "But sanctify Christ as Lord in your hearts, always being ready to make a defense to everyone who asks you to give an account for the hope that is in you, yet with gentleness and reverence." The revived Christian does not lack opportunities within his sphere of influence.

It only makes sense that God will bring people across the path of those who have consecrated their lives to being open to Christ's leading and using. Yet the Christian must still be willing to take the initiative and evangelize. The natural evangelism that occurs by revived believers living their day-to-day lives is a major means for how God desires to have us reach the lost.

When we think about revival, we often think of many lost individuals coming to Christ. Though that is not revival in itself, technically speaking, the conversion of the lost will be the natural outflow of revival. Sincere, serious Christians will impact their social circles, eventually touching their community, their nation, and the world. Much of the future impact of a faithful life is not known. Many faithful men and women have served the Lord obediently in obscurity. Yet God promises that they will have born abundant fruit. A great work of significant scope can happen when Christians bow the knee and get serious about the kingdom of God. For example, there is a great difference between a pastor who is serious about God and one who takes the position as a job. There is a great difference between a missionary who is doing social work and one that is sold out to winning souls and doing whatever Christ would ask. There is a great difference between a young person who goes along with his worldly Christian friends and a young person that stands up for Christ even at the cost of being alienated from the youth group or his circle of friends. The world is in desperate need of those who will give their all for the kingdom. We must be willing to take the initiative and stand apart. God promises to draw near to us when we draw near to Him (James 4:8). The choice is ours.

God's Roadmap for Revival

2 Chronicles 7:14 will serve as the framework for the message of this book. It says, "And My people who are called by My name humble themselves and pray and seek My face and turn from their wicked ways, then I will hear from heaven, will forgive their sin and will heal their land." 2 Chronicles 7:14 does not begin with "if" as so many placards, cards, and books like to say. The "if" is in the previous verse where God says, "If I shut up the heavens so that there is no rain, or if I command the locust to devour the land, or if I send pestilence among My people." The context for verse 14 is based upon verse 13 which is describing an instance of God's judgment upon His people for their disobedience and idolatry. In other words, if Israel became disobedient and selfish, there was still hope. God would hear, forgive, and heal their land based upon their humility, prayer, repentance, and seeking of God's face. **In other words, instead of blaming society or the times for our ineffectiveness as a church, perhaps we need to see if it is we who are responsible for God turning His face from us and thus our nation as well.** Perhaps there are sinful elements to our lives and sinful strategies to which we have aligned ourselves, and God cannot work until we repent from these sins.

We must also understand that the principle in verse 14 is given to God's people who are called by His name. If a person chooses to utilize this verse to apply to America, they are in many ways misled. The verse clearly is directed to God's people who are called by His name. In the Old Testament, that would be the Jewish nation. The New Testament application of this verse would be to the church, which consists of all who have repented and placed their trust in Jesus Christ for forgiveness, including Jews. It cannot apply to the nation of America or any other nation because it only applies to God's people who are called by His name. However, that does not mean that we cannot hold to this verse in regard to desiring this country to turn to God. Remember, the principle is that if the church is revived, the impact on society will follow. We just need to focus our thoughts upon getting right before God ourselves and then let God lead in the reformation of the nation should He choose to be so gracious.

These things said, we could restate verses 13 and 14 as follows to make them directly applicable to our time: "If I pour out judgment, harden hearts, or turn My blessing and outpouring of the Spirit away due to the disobedience of My church, and the time would come where My church would humble themselves, pray, seek My face, and turn from their wicked ways, then I will listen, forgive them, and make them a holy and shining beacon of righteousness." In other words, we need to ask God's forgiveness for where we have contributed to the lack of the Spirit's moving across our land and in our churches. We must acknowledge the areas where we have gone astray and repent. We must learn humility, how to pray, what it means to seek God's face, and have the veils taken from our eyes in some of the areas where we need to repent. Then we can expect God to respond with purification, forgiveness, renewal, and ultimately salvation for many of those lost around us.

Will He Find Faith?

There is much at stake in the question of whether a church will submit itself to the Lord's hand for a reviving work. A God Who is listening and answering prayer, a God Who is forgiving and purifying the church, and a God Who is using His church to affect change in society will be the result. This is God's promise to us. The challenge and remaining question is whether or not we will take Him seriously.

We can either avail ourselves to God's working or get in the way. The principles contained in 2 Chronicles 7:14 are relevant for all believers in all nations, so let us follow His divine directives. May God do a work that only He can do as He changes us, works in and through us, and begins to advance His kingdom on the earth in the hearts and souls of men.

Section 1:

If My People Will "Humble Themselves…"

Chapter 1:
What Really Is Humility?

"He mocks proud mockers but gives grace to the humble."
Proverbs 3:4

Humility is the starting point. If we fail here, there is no point in getting on our knees and praying for revival. No strategy will bail us out if we have a lack of humility before God. God cannot and does not fill a proud person with His Spirit. As such, there can be no spiritual power present or moving without us first being broken before God. We bring nothing to the table. We have no bargaining power and no spiritual account to draw from apart from Christ. We come empty-handed as beggars. It is only the infusion and bestowing of the grace of God that allows one beggar to serve another beggar. It is God's grace that makes revival possible. But He must first change us by His grace before others are changed.

2 Chronicles 7:13 presents a predicament for the people of God. God has poured out His wrath and punishment upon His people for their disobedient and hardened hearts. They had stiffened their neck under the discipline of God rather than becoming broken and repentant. Yet God called out to them in verse 14, reminding them that a full turn around could take place if only they would humble themselves, pray, seek His face, and turn from their wicked ways. God was ready and willing to pour out His grace, but He was waiting for His vessels to become useable.

This is always God's design. We must humble ourselves before God so that He can lift us up in due time. Humility precedes exaltation. It was true for Christ, and it is true for us.

Humility, Contrition, and Trembling

Isaiah 66:2 says, "But to this one I will look, to him who is humble and contrite of spirit, and who trembles at My word." The promise of

2 Chronicles 7:14 is available only to those who are humble, broken of spirit, and who bow their spirits before the authority of the Word of God. Contrition and trembling before the Word of God are akin to humility. Isaiah 66:2 really is not a list of three distinct spiritual realities; rather it is three different angles of observing the same truth. In other words, humility involves, by its very definition, both contrition and trembling at the Word of God. The Hebrew word for humility in 2 Chronicles 7:14, is *kana*, meaning "to bend the knee." This means to humiliate, vanquish, bring down low, bring into subjection, put under, or to subdue. Contrition, which means to repent or become ashamed of the current state of one's heart, is the immediate result of the heart which has been humbled. The humbling process will have begun with a cutting to the heart from God's Word, and it will end in a reverence and fear for the authority and supreme value of God's Word. Contrition, humility, and trembling before God's Word are the beginning point for revival. All three simultaneously exist in the humble heart.

Nehemiah 1 presents a great picture of this brokenness before God. Nehemiah was brought news of the disastrous state of affairs of his Jewish brothers back in Jerusalem. Ezra and Zerubbabel had taken some of the exiles back to Jerusalem decades before, but they were unprotected physically, spiritually lacking, and economically hurting. Upon hearing that God's people who were called by His name were in this horrendous state of affairs, Nehemiah's heart was broken to the point that he wept and mourned. He prayed and fasted for days. He acknowledged that the Jews deserved this punishment for their sin. He interceded on their behalf for forgiveness from that sin, and he offered himself as a willing vessel to be used by God to help fix the situation. He was one to whom God could look because of his broken heart. He knew despite his gifting and high position in government through which he had the king's ear that he alone couldn't fix the situation. He needed God, and that is where he started. Thus, he poured his heart out in prayer before God as a desperate man. He never stopped praying or seeking the will of God. Nehemiah didn't generate revival; rather, he was merely a vessel used of God to do God's purposes within God's story. What made him a chosen vessel of God was his tender heart. Nehemiah understood the limits of his power, influence, and ability. He understood that God alone could affect change.

For genuine revival to occur, we must become a people of tender hearts. We ought to weep over the state of affairs around us. We cannot pretend that God can send His Spirit to move if we gloss over sin issues. Sin must be identified, and it must be pursued, captured, and crushed. Some sin is obvious, while some is not. Sin relies on self, lifts up self, and operates without God and against God's ways and will. Before we can be shown such errors of spirit, we must humble ourselves to ask God to show us where we might be off course. Humility is the posture of growth because it is where God infuses His grace into a teachable spirit. Humility also has a posture of power because a bowed knee and heart which calls out to God is honored and heard by God. Humility is our starting point.

Humility bows the knee to listen to the Spirit of God, and contrition breaks the heart and will to repent and change. God's Word is the catalyst for both. We cannot read God's Word as a self-help manual or as a guidebook for how to selfishly get more out of this life. Rather, it is the authoritative revelation of God that stands in judgment over every man. No one is allowed to change one letter or punctuation point. It is firm, it endures, it convicts, it is the power of God to salvation, and it is inspired of God for our growth as believers. It cuts to the heart and convicts of sin. We must tremble before it when we read it or hear it taught. It is unlike other words on paper bound in a book. It is God-breathed, and it is living and active, even today. We must read it as such, preach it as such, and study it as such. It is not merely a collection of information, and it is not merely some really neat stories. It is equated with Christ Himself. John 1:1 says, "In the beginning was the Word, and the Word was with God, and the Word was God." Jesus Christ is the embodiment of truth. The only two things called "truth" are Jesus and the Word of God. We should tremble before Jesus, and we must also tremble before His Word. God gave it to mankind, so we need to consider it to be more than important. Do we tremble when we hear the Word of God read? Does it cut us to the heart? Do we believe that all of it is true? Do we believe that God can do the impossible and that we cannot? God has vested His power in His Word. No amount of charisma, anecdotes, or stories can take the place of the exposition of the Word of God. The Word of God unleashed by a humble and contrite preacher trembling before it will undoubtedly lead to a reviving work of God and probably some persecution.

Humility of Mind

Philippians 2:3-4 says, "Do nothing from selfishness or empty conceit, but with humility of mind regard one another as more important than yourselves; do not merely look out for your own personal interests, but also for the interests of others." This passage tells us one of the major evidences of a humble heart. If we have the humility of mind characterized by surrender, contrition, and trembling before God, then we will necessarily think of others as more important than ourselves. It doesn't say that they are more valuable than we are, for God values us all equally as His children. He is not partial. It says that we are to be cognizant of the needs and welfare of others more than we are consumed with ourselves. Humility is not a neglect of self where we act as doormats for others; rather, it is a demeanor and mindset that is far more concerned about how others are than how we ourselves are. Humility is the opposite of self-centeredness because it is driven by service for God and others.

If we find that our hearts are not broken by the eternal destiny of the lost around us or if we are not moved to pray, we are lacking in humility. True humility thinks of others as more important than ourselves. Such a humble mindset will lead to prayer, seeking God's face, and a consistency in repenting over sin. This is why it all starts with humility.

Lose Our Lives

We truly humble ourselves when we do what Christ said in Mark 8:35. After He told His disciples to deny themselves, take up their crosses, and follow Him, He said, "For whoever wishes to save his life will lose it, but whoever loses his life for My sake and the gospel's will save it." The way of the cross is to pour out our lives into the wells of others. It is to get rid of the self-focus and self-effort that characterizes all other means and systems of worship besides true Christianity. It is saying, "I can't, but He can." It is doing all things for the sake of the gospel. True humility is to lose our lives in exchange for receiving Christ's life. Paul says in Galatians 2:20, "I have been crucified with Christ; and it is no longer I who live, but Christ lives in me; and the life which I now live in the flesh I live by faith in the Son of God, who loved me and gave Himself up for me." Like Paul, we must cease to exist in our own self-centered controlling mechanisms, our own fleshly agendas, our own carnal goals, our own twisted desires, and our own egocentric choices. We must surrender them, crucify them, and by faith walk according to Christ's plans, desires, goals, and agendas for our lives. We must bow our knees before Christ, subject ourselves to do His bidding, and vanquish the flesh with all of its passions and desires.

True Humility

We try to exalt ourselves by our skills, intellect, and education, among other things. Our Lord says in 1 Peter 5:6, "Therefore humble yourselves under the mighty hand of God, that He may exalt you at the proper time." True exaltation can only be given by Christ Himself, and it will be given to those who vanquish their own selfish agendas and desires and place themselves in submission to their Master and their Lord, Jesus Christ. Like John the Baptist says in John 3:30, "He must increase, but I must decrease." We decrease not by self-abasement or self-insult but by dying to self and immersing ourselves in Christ's life, purpose, love, and power. **Life is not about discovering our purpose but surrendering to the purposes of God.** We should follow His example to disregard our rights to what we want in favor of what God wants. We should consider others are more important than ourselves, and we should be willing to humble ourselves by becoming obedient to the point of death. We are called to crucify our fleshly desires so that we can live for Christ, and we must also submit ourselves to God's plan and desires, even if it means our own death for the sake of the gospel. True humility bows the knee to the true Lord of the universe and says, "Lord, not my will but Yours be done."

Yet Satan makes it such that we can delude ourselves into thinking that we are humble when we are not. We must dig deeper.

Chapter 2:
Cease Operating on Human Strength and Ingenuity

"The things that are impossible with people are possible with God."
Luke 18:27

It is our nature to draw from our own wells, to leverage our talents, and to think as man thinks. God's ways are so often not our own, confounding the wise. The wisdom of this world amounts to foolishness before God. We must come to the place where we draw from the eternal and bottomless well of Christ Himself. He alone can affect change and do ministry. John 6:29 says, "Jesus answered and said to them, 'This is the work of God, that you believe in Him whom He has sent.'" The work of the Christian is faith. Yes, works will follow and effort must be made, but it is God doing the work in us and through us that will yield fruit that will last. God is more concerned that we bring great faith to the table than He is interested in our particular skills, degrees, and accomplishments. He can and does infuse His people with His power to do what only He can do. We are in a supernatural battle that requires supernatural authority and power.

The Example of the Disciples

Acts 4:33 says, "Now as they observed the confidence of Peter and John and understood that they were uneducated and untrained men, they were amazed, and began to recognize them as having been with Jesus." Why would God choose a dozen uneducated men? If we were put in the place of Christ, would we have gone down to the docks and found a bunch of fishermen to try to establish a heavenly kingdom? Would we have confided the wisdom of heaven in "simple" people, trusting that the gospel would reach the ends of the earth through their witness? It seems ludicrous to our minds which are saturated in Ph.D.'s, media elites, and celebrities. Our culture elevates, glorifies, and even worships those who have reached fame. We even call our pop icons "idols." We admire those who have "made it" or struck it rich. Some of the more well-meaning elites would like to tell the rest of us that if we just tried hard enough, worked hard enough, and waited long enough, we could achieve what they did and be who they are, or at least something comparable. Most of us live constantly hoping to be like somebody else or to please somebody else. Yet the reality is that Christ was looking for something beyond exterior appearances of success and worldly achievement. He was looking at the heart, and He chose those whom the world would not have chosen.

Paul was educated and an intellectual elite, and it took blindness and a humbling direct encounter with God to get through to him. The rest of the disciples were not "successes" like Paul was when he was the Pharisee Saul. In fact, they were seeking any way that they could become great, especially in the kingdom of Christ. Mark 9:33-35 says,

> "They came to Capernaum; and when He was in the house, He began to question them, 'What were you discussing on the way?' But they kept silent, for on the way they had discussed with one another which of them was the greatest. Sitting down, He called the twelve and said to them, 'If anyone wants to be first, he shall be last of all and servant of all.'"

Jesus' response to His disciples was to instruct them that it is those who are the servants of others who will be greatest in the life to come. His challenge to His disciples was that they would develop a changed mindset that accepted lowliness and that they wouldn't set their hearts upon worldly fame, recognition, and success. We must come to the point where we no longer are self-seeking and self-promoting but rather self-denying and others-serving. There is nothing wrong with desiring rewards in heaven and in being given great honor there. The sin is to try to impress everybody now and to get all that we can out of the world system now. And for those who do have a lot of God-given status and ability, they must use it to do a lot of service, for God will hold them accountable according to what they have been given. The challenge for them in particular is that God must teach them to use their positions and abilities with His strength, power, and energy and not their own. If they do not come to understand that anything that they do that bears fruit for the kingdom is a result of Christ in them, they will become boastful and arrogant, self-sufficient, and self-seeking. God needs humble hearts that are pliable in His hands.

We can take heart that Jesus chose weak people like the disciples to do His kingdom work. Though they made a lot of mistakes, they were teachable. The real change happened when the Holy Spirit came at Pentecost. The "simple" disciples, the uneducated fisherman, were suddenly transformed into bold witnesses for Christ. There was no more pursuing status or cowering in shame at being identified with Christ. They became bold spokesmen for Christ, seeking the welfare of others for their eternal state, beyond just their earthly state. These are those to whom God entrusted the kingdom. When they operated on their own power and authority, they were bumbling fools and powerless, being rebuked by Christ for a lack of faith. When the Holy Spirit indwelt them and filled them, they were changed men, able to stand up before a hostile crowd and declare the eternal truth of the gospel without fear or cowering. There was no denying that they knew Christ, but rather there was a joyous identification and fellowship in His suffering. The Spirit's indwelling, empowering, and filling was clearly what gave them the ability to be the testimonies that they were. We can be thankful that He has given us His Holy Spirit so that in our weakness He can show Himself strong and powerful. This is our only hope, and thus we must make our boast in Him.

Strength in Weakness

Paul experienced some wonderful heavenly visions in his life. Such a special experience could have easily made him proud, so God allowed a minister of Satan to afflict him. What that was doesn't matter as much as that we understand that it caused him some real pain and strife. It brought him enough difficulty, in fact, to keep him humble and drawing from the Lord's resources and power. Paul says in 2 Corinthians 12:9, "And He has said to me, 'My grace is sufficient for you, for power is perfected in weakness.' Most gladly, therefore, I will rather boast about my weaknesses, so that the power of Christ may dwell in me."

The obvious truth from this passage is that God's power is more clearly evident when presented through a weak vessel, like having a great treasure in a jar of clay. The treasure is what shines bright and gets the recognition, not the outer covering which is weak and in decay. But a deeper truth presents itself as well that many miss. **Not only is Christ more clearly seen in weakness, but He often chooses to work in weakness to accomplish His will. It is here that power is perfected, not merely made clearer.**

Power Comes in Identification with Christ

There is a labor by the Spirit and of the Spirit and a labor according to the flesh and empowered by fleshly, carnal energy. One is self-based and the other is founded upon the strength of Christ. If we sow after the flesh, we will reap accordingly. If we sow after the Spirit, we can reap a fruitful harvest. There is much Christian labor that depends upon the flesh rather than the Spirit. Only God knows the heart, but here are possible examples. There is a pastor who tries to keep people paying attention to his sermon by trying really hard to vary his voice fluctuations and use arm movements rather than relying upon the sufficiency of the Word of God and the enabling of the Spirit. There is a fleshly energy and a spiritual one. From the outside, they can look exactly the same. God must search the heart. There is a Bible study leader who is very likeable and charismatic. He builds bridges to people with great interpersonal skills and gets them excited to be around other Christians. Is he using fleshly, natural abilities to do the work of God, or is He yielded to the Spirit who is enabling him to supernaturally love others? It is either a really good Christian performance based in the strength of self or it is a miracle of Christ working in his heart. Only God knows. This is the dichotomy which we must dissect if we are to understand true humility and surrender. God must speak to our hearts to show us where we are failing to draw from His strength alone.

Christ doesn't need big spiritual muscles and a master of theology degree to do His work. Discipline, degrees, and abilities are great. They are not wrong or evil. But like leaning on self-effort and self-righteousness for salvation, we too can be tempted to lean upon self-effort and self-advancement for ministry and sanctification. God must deal with our hearts to show us how to be drawing from His resources throughout all of life, not merely when we are in a difficult predicament or a time of trial. It really is a matter of where we choose to put our trust, our confidence, and our ultimate reliance. We put it either in ourselves or in Christ. **Operating in the flesh includes not just when we indulge our sinful desires but also when we fail to live by faith because we rely upon ourselves.** We are either consumed with ourselves or with Christ. Of course, we must only be consumed with Christ.

Too often, Christians resort to using secular resources as their guide. It is even possible that we spend too much effort reading "Christian" books rather than studying the Bible itself. And when we do read the Bible, too often we make it academic instead of supernatural and spiritual. It becomes mostly about our brain interacting with information rather than God's Word by the Holy Spirit's work cutting to our hearts. Life in Christ does not consist solely of information. The kingdom consists not in words but in power (1 Corinthians 4:20). This is not to say that we are not to use reason, logic, and sound thinking. God gave us brains for a reason. The point is that we must realize that we need pure hearts and sensitivity to the Spirit's work in our hearts in order to properly learn God's Word, develop sound theology, and make right practical day to day decisions. We are dependent upon the Spirit, whether we realize it or not and whether we heed His conviction or not.

Proverbs 16:9 says, "In his heart a man plans his course, but the LORD determines his steps." There is nothing wrong with planning, but we must not ultimately rely upon our own ability to plan as if we are in ultimate control of our future. If God is honored by our faith, does it take more faith to follow our plans for years in advance or to listen to how God is working moment by moment and day by day? Surely it is not wrong to have an idea in our minds of what we would like to see happen, or else it is nearly impossible to make decisions in a given day. Without an idea of what our lives and ministries are all about, we will flounder in the daily grind. But we must ask ourselves if we are taking everything to the Lord in prayer or if we only pray about those things which we do not as of yet have under control. God wants control of everything. No part of our heart or mind is exempt.

We must learn to let Christ work *in and through* us to accomplish *His* work. Too often our focus is misplaced, having been put on us and on our working for God rather than letting the power of Christ work in and through us by faith. Paul said in Galatians 2:20, "It is no longer I who live, but Christ lives in me." As Ephesians 2:8-9 says, we were saved by grace through faith, something not of ourselves so that we wouldn't boast. Yet too often we live the Christian life not through faith or by grace because we too often operate as self-dependent beings. It is no wonder that we have an ego problem among many "successful" pastors and Christians. The church in America is littered with self-sufficiency. God will humble us if we do not humble ourselves.

2 Corinthians 4:7 says, "But we have this treasure in jars of clay to show that this all-surpassing power is from God and not from us." The power to change lives is from God and not from us. Why are we so worried about empowering us with us or some other fleshly strategy, enterprise, or idea? It is God Who does the work. It is God Who has the all-surpassing power. Why do we try to paint, sculpt, and beautify the vessel when it is God who wants to be seen and Who is more clearly seen when the vessel is weak, cracked, and broken? This is the error in any self-help, feel good psychology solution. We need to let Christ be our life and strength rather than trying to fortify our own failing humanness and flesh. Self must be denied, not resurrected and fortified. God's strength is perfected in weakness. It is in that that we must boast. Any other boast is an insult to God. God working powerfully and supernaturally through our frailty is a testimony to the glory and grace of God. It is no coincidence that Paul mentioned that not many of the highly gifted or of high society were part of the church (1 Corinthians 1:26). Christ said that it was nearly impossible for a wealthy person to enter heaven (Matthew 19:23). The more capable we are or the more status we have, the harder it is to get self out of the way. There are exceptions, of course, but it is no accident that God chooses to work through the weak to show Himself strong. He wants all the glory.

Apart from Christ we can do nothing (John 15:5). It is an all or nothing deal. Either we are alive in Christ, or we are not. Either we are abiding, or we are not. Either we are accomplishing spiritual things for the kingdom, or we are not. It all hinges upon whether we are by faith leaning totally on His power for any change to be accomplished. It is so hard for the strong, powerful, successful, and wise person to see this truth. Perhaps that is why Christ chose fishermen. They were not likely to have a strong pride problem. He chose the weak, and through His empowering they became strong witnesses for the kingdom. Just because we are saved does not mean that we automatically operate in Christ's wisdom and power. We must first believe that we have no wisdom of ourselves, and we must by faith seek and access Christ's wisdom and power. Christ doesn't want to be prayed to only when tough times come. He wants us to draw from His well of Living Water at all times.

Christ ought to be manifested in us and through us, and He ought to be our very life. Colossians 3:3 says, "For you have died and your life is hidden with Christ in God." In case that is not clear enough, Paul continues in verse four saying, "When Christ, who is our life, is revealed, then you also will be revealed with Him in glory." Christ literally lives within us. He is to be our very life. Spiritually speaking, we are His very body, He being the head. There is a mystical spiritual union that is of the utmost importance. Of course we do not cease to exist as individuals with independent minds, wills, and hearts, but it is a matter of not drawing from our own fleshly strength to do ministry. It is giving our hearts to God to do as He wishes. The common thing for Christians to do is to do what we want how we want and when we want and get Christ's stamp of approval on our agenda. Christ doesn't play that game. He wants to set the course and be our very life and ministry. We have no life apart from life in Christ and being one with Him, drawing from His infinite resources and eternal power.

A True Surrender

Some Christians don't even attempt to surrender all areas of their lives to Christ. This, at best, makes them double-minded, unstable, a poor testimony, and of little use to the kingdom. At worst, they may need to reevaluate their salvation. On the other hand, there are many Christians who think that they have surrendered all to Christ. But we need to ask ourselves if we have ever truly given up all dreams, ambitions, desires, plans, aspirations, and goals, and said, "I will do whatever You want me to do this day, and tomorrow I will seek You in the same way." Have we come to the end of ourselves spiritually? We must pray that God would show us what it means to let Christ live in us and to give up total control of our lives. The process of God breaking us and refining us is typically not smooth, fun, or easy, but coming to His desired place of total surrender is a place of true freedom and total joy.

How different is this kind of thinking from that which is common among Christian leaders today? They say that we should come up with the biggest dream for our lives or for the kingdom and seize it. Whatever happened to God's will? What does God want? Who will get the glory if we make a business venture for the kingdom and succeed? It will be we who get the glory and recognition and even worship, which is exactly what is happening in American Christianity.

These truths about humility and surrender are difficult ones to appropriate. Indeed, even their appropriation will be done by the grace of God through faith. Yet there is no other way. We cannot beat our flesh into submission, we cannot educate ourselves into surrender, nor can we discipline our minds and wills to exercise a spirit of lowliness. It must be a work of God in us and through us by faith. There is no three-step plan for success or seven habits of highly effective Christians. **We really do have to let God bring us to our knees.** We really do have to surrender and come to the end of ourselves. Like Jacob, we are stubborn by nature, wrestling God day after day so that we can get our way and tell Him how we want our lives to be. Yet may God, as He did with Jacob, touch us and bring us to brokenness and defeat before Him. Then we can find true strength in our weakness, even if it means that we go through life with a limp like Jacob did. True life and freedom in Christ requires that His very will, desires, and goals are ours as well. **God doesn't exist to help us with our agenda, but we exist to cooperate with His agenda.**

Proverbs 3:5-6 says, "Trust in the LORD with all your heart, and *do not lean on your own understanding*. In all your ways acknowledge Him, and He will make your paths straight" (emphasis added). A good intellect is a gift from God, but a gifted person cannot depend upon his or her giftedness to do the work of the kingdom or to determine the will of God. We must trust completely in God, leaning upon Him. Understanding is fine, but we cannot lean on it. The only true foundation is Christ. **It takes a humble person to put His entire spiritual investment in God's fund.** We should pray and work knowing that it all depends upon the power, strength, and wisdom of Christ in us.

We can never do something for God. Rather, God does His work through us when we surrender to His desires and plan for our lives. For example, at many church meetings, a quick prayer is often said to bless the meeting or items on the agenda, but rarely is God sought for the agenda itself. He is asked to bless our work rather than being the One doing the work in and through us to His glory. There is nothing wrong with seeking God's blessing, but we must understand that the only work that God blesses is the work that He does, not anything that we can conjure up on our own. We need His strength, power, and wisdom, for therein lies the blessing itself.

Psalm 127:1 says, "Unless the Lord builds the house, those who build it labor in vain." A huge budget and building program don't guarantee fruitfulness. If and when God builds the man or His church, we can be assured of a harvest. We must understand that even service for God can be filled with pride and lead us to more pride if we have yet to understand and embrace our own weakness apart from Christ. God wants us to pray because prayer casts us upon God, but He is against prayer that does not truly come from hearts open to the mind of God. A true and total surrender makes a huge difference.

Day by Day Living

Living in surrender to God and walking by faith is not a silly thing where we must stop and recite a prayer before every minor decision. It is, however, a way of being that asks of every decision, "What does God want right now in this?" God gave Israel manna each day, enough for that day or that day plus the Sabbath day. He gives what we need when we need it and typically no more. This is why He commands us to pray to God that He would give us our daily bread, not our weekly, monthly, or a decade's worth of bread. It is a mindset and a different existence that is utterly cast upon God because there is no other option and no other way can work because of how weak and fallible we are left to ourselves. We need God.

Practically Speaking

The Biblical truth is that human solutions are not solutions to spiritual problems. In other words, if there is a lack of God-honoring prayer in a person's church, the human solution might be to get the elders together and brainstorm solutions. Then the list could be narrowed, pros and cons could be listed, and then the best option could be chosen. Then the meeting could be adjourned by thanking God for giving His wisdom and solving the problem. But God had nothing to do with the solution. His wisdom was not sought. The elders should be praised and thanked for their labor and great minds, though they should not be praised for their spirituality.

Some fleshly solutions are obviously human-driven while some are more Biblically enshrouded. To get people interested in preaching, a human solution might be to shorten a message because people nowadays can't concentrate as long as they used to, or so people say. To get more people to come to church, the church service could be altered to be appealing to their selfish emotions and desires. To get more people to serve, they can be guilt-tripped by the pastor each and every Sunday. To motivate people to accept Christ and come to the front of the sanctuary, the same chorus can be sung over and over, each time at one key higher and a bit louder, trying to assuage the emotions which could in turn manipulate the will. Many human solutions are nothing other than Satanic tricks and manmade gimmicks. They sound good and reasonable at first glance, and many get taken by them for years or even a lifetime.

Sometimes a human solution is something that is not directly forbidden in the Bible. Perhaps a pastor decides to launch a Sunday School program. Was that his idea or did He seek the will of God in the matter? The answer to that question will determine whether the solution was spiritual in nature or fleshly. Solutions must be according to the Word of God, and they must be Spirit-led. If they are not, who is leading them? If it is not God, it can only be the devil. It is one or the other. As Matthew 6:24 says, we cannot serve God and wealth (or the devil) at the same time. We cannot solve spiritual problems with human solutions, good or bad, effective or ineffective. **Whether or not something generates apparent results can never be used to justify the spirituality of a program, person, or church.**

The only true solution comes in identifying the spiritual issue that has gone wrong. Leaders must pray to have spiritual discernment, they must ask God to show them how to encourage or admonish others to commit to prayer, and they must set an example of Spirit-led prayer themselves. They need to ask God for wisdom (see Proverbs 2:1-9). These are spiritual means to solve spiritual problems because they are based upon trusting in God and leaning upon Him for direction and answers.

It is becoming endemic that churches use solutions sprung from human effort and ingenuity to solve problems. If we are deficient in leadership, we look to effective worldly leaders to show us how to lead. There are plenty of effective leaders in the Scriptures, so why not look there? Is God's Word insufficient? If our praise and worship time is dull, we try to liven it up with a peppier song. Is it simply an emotional issue or is a deeper heart issue to blame? If people don't want to listen to a sermon, we try to make church more entertaining. Naturally, people would rather be told what they think they need to hear. As long as they are told what they want to hear, they stay. Tell them the truth, and they go. We had better tell the truth. Proclaiming the truth is always a spiritual solution as long as it is done in faith, humility, and gentleness.

People are encouraged to come to Christ when they see our love, unity, holiness, good works, and these kinds of authentic spiritual, supernatural things. Somebody's church building might be old and their congregation devoid of musical talent. Human wisdom would say to hire a gifted musician and get a new building. Spiritual wisdom very well may say, "So what? We worship God in spirit and truth even if it is off key and sometimes with no instruments. But we love God and others. His Word is being proclaimed by a pastor who is vibrant in his faith and gifted to teach." Biblically, couldn't a person find Christ through His proclaimed Word and through Christians who live out Christ in their lives, even if some of the outer material things are lacking? Absolutely! God's strength is perfected in our weakness. This is not a denunciation of good music or nice buildings. It is a denunciation of churches who think that, unless we have these things, we can never reach people with the gospel. That is beyond false. The unsaved are reached by revived Christians and God releasing His Spirit to move. They are not drawn to Christ (though maybe to church) by emotional manipulation or material items. Let us not lure people to church by appealing to fleshly appetites, but may we attract them by our consecrated, committed, and contagious lives in Christ.

Spiritual Preaching

It is imperative that preachers preach as the Spirit leads according to sound study of the Word. They must preach the full counsel of God and not cater to the "felt need" deception, where preaching is said to be helpful only if it adheres to what people think they need to hear. The problem with that thinking is that it is *the truth* that we need to hear, and only it will set us free. Too often we are deceived into sinning, and we need the Word of God to cut us to the heart to show us what our real needs are, whether we feel them or not. There is no substitute for truth, and there is no saving or sanctifying message other than the Word of God. Jesus prayed in John 17:17 to the Father, "Sanctify them in the truth; Your word is truth." We are not sanctified by appealing to our fleshly desires for what we think we need. We are brought into relationship with God through the truth of the Word of God.

Romans 1:16 says, "For I am not ashamed of the gospel for it is the power of God unto salvation for the Jew first and also the Greek." The gospel is the power of God for salvation for all men and for all times and places. When Paul ministered in Athens, those people had no clue about God. Yet the gospel in its fullness was the message that they needed to hear. Religious background or no religious background, the Word of God and the gospel of God is what must be heard and understood. Nothing else will change a life and heart. The gospel and the Word of God are powerful in all times and in all cultures. People change, times change, and societies changes, but the Word of the Lord endures forever. It must be read publicly, preached entirely, and submitted to fully. Like Paul at Athens, we ought to try to make a connection, but it is always through the Word that God will bring us truth and affect change. Fleshly preaching is concerned about results and how the audience receives the message. Messages are classified based upon how well they were received, not based upon how true they were to the Word. Spiritual preaching says what God's Word says and leaves the results with God. Spiritual preaching's chief concern is, "What does God's Word say and how does the Spirit want us to apply it?" The spiritual preacher then lets the Spirit enable him in his study and preparation and empower him in his delivery.

A Spiritual Gathering

It is incomprehensible that some churches begin by surveying the community and seeing what it will take to get people to come to church, and then they craft a church to meet the wants and desires of what the unsaved people think that they need. The problem with this thinking is that the natural man is not spiritually discerned; they couldn't possibly know what they need in and of themselves. Consider 1 Corinthians 2:14 which says, "But a natural man does not accept the things of the Spirit of God, for they are foolishness to him; and he cannot understand them, because they are spiritually appraised." How can we trust in what the individual who lacks spiritual discernment thinks church should be like? It makes absolutely no sense to ask unregenerate people who are yet dead in the heart and held captive by Satan what they think should draw them to church. We already know what draws the unsaved: love, unity, good works, holiness, hope, and so on, according to the leading and drawing of the Spirit. God has given us the road map. We don't need to ask, and we certainly don't need to ask the lost. That is why they are called lost. They don't know where they are going, and they cannot perceive what is right. The Holy Spirit must work in them to illumine their minds and guide them into truth according to the Scriptures. Faith comes by hearing the Word of God, and nothing else will work to generate faith.

If we want to share the gospel with someone, we should live a life of purity before them, love them, pray for them, and share the gospel with them as the Lord leads. There is nothing wrong with inviting them to church, for certainly the gospel permeates everything that the church is about, or at least it should. They should be able to see that church is not about lifeless sermons, potlucks with unfriendly people, kids running about out of control, organ music only, and being nice. They need to see true love and how God's Word is still totally relevant for today.

Conclusions

God's Word says in 1 Corinthians 1:28-29, "And the base things of the world and the despised God has chosen, the things that are not, so that He may nullify the things that are, so that no man may boast before God." For reasons that only God knows completely, He has chosen what is weak to glorify Himself and to make the worldly-wise look foolish. All men, upon realizing this, will be humbled before God, having nothing to boast of.

We can do nothing to please God on our own. We stand, or rather bow, humbled because of what Christ has done in already overcoming the world and conquering death. He has already lived the perfect life. In Him alone are all power and wisdom and knowledge. Yet somehow we think that we have some of this stuff. We think we are pretty savvy, but we are fools to think so. Our entire identity and worth is tied up in Christ, for we are nothing and have nothing apart from Him. Ephesians 1:22-24 says, "And He put all things in subjection under His feet, and gave Him as head over all things to the church, which is His body, the fullness of Him who fills all in all." We are in subjection to Christ, for He is our Head. It is high time we start asking Him what He wants and get ourselves off His throne. He fills all in all, and there is no room left for us to brag or boast. This is His time, and our lives are His to use. Our churches are His to lead, and we must humble ourselves and submit to His plans. We must admit our weakness, embrace His strength, and surrender to His authority. Only then can we be empowered with His might.

This is why we must cease operating on human strength and ingenuity. We are Christ's, and He possesses all strength and ingenuity. This means that we don't have any. We think we do because we are thinking in human terms. 2 Corinthians 10:3-4 says, "For though we walk in the flesh, we do not war according to the flesh, for the weapons of our warfare are not of the flesh, but divinely powerful for the destruction of fortresses." Even though we are human, the battles we fight and the lives we live must be superhuman; that is, they must be of the Spirit, tapping into the divine resources within us in Christ. **To accomplish spiritual things in a spiritual way we need spiritual power which is found only in Christ.** We need Him. Let us draw from His overflowing well of grace, mercy, strength, and power. **May we let Him be our strength as we realize by faith that we have none.**

Chapter 3:
Surrender Absolutely to God's Authority

"It is the Lord Christ whom you serve." Colossians 3:24

The pendulum in the American church has swung from an emphasis on Jesus as Lord and Savior to merely Jesus as Savior. Formerly, the emphasis was on a holy, righteous God Who will pour out His wrath on unrighteous sinners and Who disciplines His children who walk in sin. Presently, the focus is on the fact that God is loving, good, and merciful, all of which are totally true. However, a complete understanding of Who God is requires an emphasis on both. The love and mercy of God only makes sense and carries power in light of our sin, which makes us fall short of His perfect standard. If the wrath of God is not taught, the love of God comes across as a mere tolerance and overlooking of sin.

Too many churches teach a reductionist gospel, one that carries the least offense and isn't even rooted directly in Biblical truth. People are told that God has a wonderful plan for their lives, which to a carnal mind would mean that God will make their lives go smoothly. So they try God out and ride the bandwagon until the ride gets too bumpy. Others are told that they have a God-shaped hole in their heart that only God can fill. This is true in a sense, but some people are satiated by their fleshly desires. They are not interested in trying something else. Others try it to see what kind of buzz Jesus can provide. In these marginally Biblical interpretations of the gospel, God becomes an attempt for the unbeliever to fortify their own flesh and make their lives work out how they would prefer.

We have lost the idea that God hates sin. Our culture doesn't tolerate the notion of sin and the wrath of God. Yet that is the message that must be preached. We must carefully show people that they have violated the righteous standards of God, whether they believe in them or not, and we must take them to the cross which is the only solution for their being forgiven. **The emphasis needs to be placed back upon the fact that the unsaved person needs to be made righteous and not happy.**

The gospel is offensive because it shows people that they have sinned. We cannot get around that fact because there is no need for a Savior if we are not sinners. Repentance is required to enter the kingdom. This is the message that Jesus preached, saying, "Repent for the kingdom of heaven is at hand" (Matthew 4:17). The apostles preached that people would repent and be saved (Acts 3:19). Jesus is not a Savior without repentance. We need to teach people that Jesus desires to be Lord of their lives and that He wants to be on the throne of their hearts. Many people think that they are saved because they said some magic formula or prayed a certain prayer. A mere profession that Christ is Savior is not sufficient. Even the demons believe that Jesus is God, and they shudder (James 2:19). Yet many professing Christians fail to tremble or even recognize the holiness of God. A profession of faith must lead to a possession of faith in Christ, a complete anchoring and relying solely upon the merits of Christ. Where is the trembling before God for mercy and forgiveness? Where is desire to get rid of the old and get on with the new? Where is the surrender of living for self unto living for Christ? We cannot lose the essence of the gospel of fleeing the wrath that is to come.

James 2:26 teaches us that "faith without works is dead." Those who profess Christianity but have little in the way of a changed life to show for it need to examine themselves to see if they are of the faith (2 Corinthians 13:5). Is there a conviction of the Spirit immediately upon having sinned? When sin does happen, is there a consistency of confessing sin before God? If neither is true, there is reason to question salvation.

Core to the gospel message is the reality of Jesus as Lord of our lives. Perhaps we only understand initially that Jesus saved us from our sin, but, as we grow in Christ, we ought to quickly learn that our trusting in Jesus for salvation also implies that we are to live for Him in this life. Sadly, professing Christians sinning without conviction or godly sorrow is pandemic. This has got to change if revival is to come. Jesus must be the Savior of our hearts and the Lord of our lives. We were once slaves of sin, but Christ has set us free to be slaves of righteousness. He is Lord and Master, and we are His slaves, like it or not. There are no other options. We must return to preaching a fully Biblical gospel, and we must give Christians teaching adequate to guide them into Christlike living by the grace of God according to the work of the Spirit within them.

A Total Commitment

One definition of revival could be when a Christian makes a total commitment to God. Part of sanctification is God showing us what parts of us are not yet surrendered or consecrated to Him. This is God's reviving work in our lives, especially if we have fallen from where we had formerly been.

When we talk of a total commitment to God, which is a complete selling out to His will and a surrendering to His purposes, we need to understand that it is by the grace of God. In an effort to generate personal revival, we would naturally begin to think of all the spiritual disciplines that we could train ourselves to do. We might try to read the Bible more, pray more, memorize more Scripture, and so on. These are all wonderful as long as the focus does not become self and as long as self-effort does not become the means to attempting to grow spiritually. Growth and revival can only happen through a reliance upon Christ and from a drawing by faith upon His gracious resources and power. We can't work up a total commitment; rather, Christ must sovereignly bring us low.

Spiritual growth will happen ultimately only by faith. Hudson Taylor, the well-known missionary to China, said, "How to get faith strengthened? Not by a striving after faith, but by resting on the Faithful One." For years he was in internal misery because he couldn't discipline himself to maintain a restful and fully committed Christian walk. He was the master of spiritual disciplines, putting most of us to utter shame. He eventually realized that the way to spiritual growth and sanctification is by resting upon the One Who has promised to sanctify us completely and to finish the work in us which He alone has begun. So when we talk of a total commitment, we are talking of a faith that rests in the security of the promises of God. This means that we rely upon Him for everything and that we give up our own agendas for His perfect plan. Such a faith will be manifested in works, but they will be of a different nature. They will be because of a want-to mentality and because of an internal spiritual craving for truth, direction, wisdom, and fellowship with God. For example, we will not have a devotional time because somebody has told us to or because it is a good idea but because we desperately know we need it. It will be our heart's desire to know God and love Him more fully. And this will motivate us to pray, evangelize, and go to worship together. The motivation is completely different. Rather than trying to work to advance our standing with God, we will learn to rest in His completed work of salvation and in His ongoing work of sanctification which He also will complete.

As we rest in the Faithful One and draw near to God, God will draw us to His Word and to His heart in prayer. He will move us to share our faith as He breaks our hearts for the lost. Our hearts will ache over how the church is becoming like the world. When we draw near to God in faith, He will draw near to us (James 4:8). This is His promise to us if only we will take Him up on it. If we are afraid of what He might tell us or show us, we are in all the more dire need to call to Him.

It is not uncommon to hear professing Christians say that they are just not interested in growing in their relationship with God. In fact, some go so far as to say that they are not interested in God at all, and their lives bear evidence of that. They show no evidence of the agony of unconfessed sin that David so graphically admitted to in Psalm 51. It is difficult to understand how they can be so casual about disregarding the Lord of the universe, especially if He is indeed the Lord of their hearts. Yet others admit that they are not walking with God as they ought to, but they desire change. That is a respectable and godly desire, yet the move is theirs. Sometimes such comments are made as if it is God's fault that they are not completely sold out and on fire for God. The principle for revival is that we (as God gives us grace) make the first move to draw near to God. The fact that many Christians live lives devoid of commitment and passion forces us, based upon James 4:8, to conclude that it is their own fault. It is not God's fault, as if He has not sent some sign or movement of the Spirit that is required to live revived lives. We have the Spirit within our hearts desperately calling to us to be revived, if indeed He does indwell us. The reality is that we are, in a sense, suppressing and repressing the Spirit. We grieve the Spirit when we ought to be grieving over unconfessed sin in our hearts and in the hearts of others. How can this be turned around? What has become clear is that we must educate even professing Christians as to what the gospel is all about. We must then move to teach them how to study the Bible. Few take it literally, seriously, and authoritatively anymore. It has become merely a list of helpful hints and suggestions to get the most out of life. Some don't even bother to dissect the Scriptures, arguing that only the gospel matters. Scripture says of itself that all of it is for our training in righteousness (2 Timothy 3:16-17). The things written in earlier times were for our instruction (Romans 15:4). We must seek to understand and study the whole counsel of God, for that is part and parcel to the Great Commission (Matthew 28:19-20). Revival will never occur if we undermine the absolute power, authority, sufficiency, and infallibility of the Word of God. We must cling to every word. If not every word mattered, why would God threaten to curse someone who changed even the smallest part of a word (Revelation 22:18-19, Deuteronomy 4:2)?

If a person seriously desires to be revived and to fully commit his life to Christ, he must ask God to take total control of his life by faith. It is that simple. If such a prayer is prayed in faith, God will answer it and show Himself powerful and faithful.

A Serious Discipleship

What does a revived person look like? What are we supposed to be revived to? How can we know if a person has genuinely been revived? The answer is simply to return to what God originally called us to be. When Christ chose the twelve disciples, He came to them with an all or nothing mentality. This wasn't a try-it-and-see-if-you-like-it deal, it wasn't a dabbling in casual Christianity, nor was it an offering of a part-time employment or a short-term spiritual contract. Jesus says in Luke 14:26, "If anyone comes to Me, and does not hate his own father and mother and wife and children and brothers and sisters, yes, and even his own life, he cannot be My disciple." He is not talking here about a suicidal mentality, nor is He telling us to literally despise our family and reject them for life. He is painting a graphic picture of what genuine discipleship will require. Jesus is saying that our families might reject us, we will be ridiculed, we will suffer, and the life and image and popularity that we once had will be gone. When we give it all up to follow Christ, we cannot expect people to applaud or to understand. They will think we have lost it, that we have joined an extreme movement, and that we are radicals. We will go so far as to tell them that we are right and that they are wrong. We will even tell them kindly but boldly that everlasting punishment awaits them if they do not repent. We will be ridiculed and become nuisances in what was formerly a Christian culture. Persecution will likely come even from many professing believers if we take everything in the Scriptures seriously. Are we willing to accept this? How many of us when we prayed to receive Christ and repented of our sinful ways really understood the high stakes that Christ was setting before us? We clearly knew that we wanted to escape hell and go to heaven, but did we really grasp that Jesus never made serious discipleship an option?

Self Must Be Denied

Mark 8:34 says, "And He summoned the crowd with His disciples, and said to them, 'If anyone wishes to come after Me, he must deny himself, and take up his cross and follow Me.'" Obviously Jesus wasn't trying to win a popularity contest, nor was He too worried about keeping the thrill-seekers on His bandwagon. He didn't water down in any way what it meant to be a follower of the Christ. A follower of Christ, He says, must deny himself, take up his cross, and follow Him.

We have all kinds of books in our culture that place the focus on ourselves. An entire section at major bookstores falls under the genre of self-help. We have one thing figured out: we need help. What we have wrong is what the human race has had wrong for thousands of years: we think we can fix the problem ourselves. Jesus gives those who are preoccupied with themselves a new and radical perspective, one which certainly isn't acceptable in our culture and likely not in the Jewish culture at that time either. He says that a follower of Jesus must deny himself. Too many teach that the answer to discouragement and depression is to boost self-esteem, a pop psychology concept. The Bible teaches to find worth and dignity in Christ and to repent of any pent up bitterness and anger. Others teach that we must love ourselves, a close cousin of esteeming self. Jesus tells us to love as He loved which was to lay down His life, to *not* esteem it, and to deny all sinful impulses. His place in heaven He did not esteem so highly as to grasp it firmly

(Philippians 2:6), but He laid down His rights to become one of us and die brutally and in a humiliating manner for the sins of the world. Jesus' ways are backwards. The church must take a radical stand against the self-esteem lie, and we must teach that we find our worth in Christ. He didn't die for us because we were worthy of His love; He died for us because He chose to love us out of His mercy and because of His desire to make us holy. We must deny and eradicate this preoccupation with self and self-advancement. Self needs to be crucified- end of story.

Biblically, self is synonymous with the flesh. The flesh is the embodiment of all of the sinful impulses and passions. Operating in the flesh can also involve any religious self-effort or carnality. The flesh can be well-disciplined, but if it is still self-strengthened, it is still flesh. Our only hope is the strength which Christ supplies. Only from the vine of Christ can the branch bear fruit that lasts. Flesh can produce numbers and professions, but it cannot produce fruit. Thus, flesh, both the illicit sinful passions and the well-adjusted flesh strengthened in religious carnality, must be reckoned dead in Christ.

The lust of the flesh is how the world operates. The flesh must be reckoned dead, self must be denied, and the life of Christ must become our very life. Our culture and sadly many in the church are not interested in a message of self-denial. Too many are interested in doing whatever it takes to make them happy because they think they are entitled to it. Jesus' words say to lose our lives for His sake. It is radical but it is true. Only then can we find true happiness.

We Must Take Up Our Cross

To take up our cross is a word picture. When a person was to be crucified he had to pick up his own cross and carry it to where he would be crucified. It was an emblem of suffering and shame, as the old chorus suggests. Crucifixion was the ultimate in suffering and in public humiliation. Yet when Christ went to the cross and was reviled, He did not revile (1 Peter 2:23). He did not resist, argue, complain, or fight back. He willingly went as a sheep to the slaughter. He modeled for us what it means to daily take up our crosses. Each day we role play Christ in our social circles. We carry our crosses metaphorically in how we are not self-absorbed, in how we esteem others as more important than ourselves, and in willingly and gladly, without complaining, taking flack for being a follower of Christ. Christ was the Suffering Servant. When we take up our cross, we invite suffering for Christ as a blessing. As Christ said, "Blessed are those who are persecuted for the sake of righteousness" (Matthew 5:10).

Too often it seems the church in America will do anything to become popular, to not offend, to find common ground with other religious groups, or to give only the one side of the gospel about the promise of life, blessing, and joy. If Jesus was trying to sell a religion, He wasn't doing a very good job. His religion required that His followers would live as if they were going to be crucified each and every day. They were to stop self-seeking and lay down their dreams for the welfare of others and for the sake of the gospel. They were to preach the message like fools and rejoice in suffering and mockery. This is radical and unique, and it is the call for us today.

Also implied in this command to take up our crosses is a reminder that our strength is found in Christ and not in ourselves. Intellectually, we would think that going through life carrying a cross would slow us down and make us a burden (Matthew 11:30). Yet Christ says that if we take His yoke upon us that His burden is light and easy. We must believe that Christ can accomplish far more than we can of ourselves. In fact, He can do anything, while we can do nothing.

We Must Follow Christ

Lastly, we are told to follow Christ. We must obey God by living according to the revealed Word of God. Psalm 119:9 says, "How can a young man keep his way pure? By keeping it according to Your word." The more we know God's Word, the more we will know how to follow Christ. It is as simple as that.

The Bond-servant Mentality

A true disciple of Christ is not the person who names the name of Christ when the spiritual weather is fair but when persecution will certainly arise. He lives for righteousness even when every emotion, temptation, and fleshly desire prompts him to do otherwise. He lives a life of service, sacrifice, and surrender. His goal is to serve and give and love because he knows that is what he is called to do and that is what others truly need. It is in his relationship to Christ and in this alone that he finds the fullness of joy. A true disciple of Christ denies himself and gives up control. He desires, seeks, and follows God's will for every area of his life, and he sacrifices to put the interests of others ahead of his own. Given this list of the costs of discipleship, is it no wonder that so few ever choose to live in such a way? When a person is living in this way, or is at least moving in such a direction, we may consider him to have been revived.

This true discipleship is illustrated Biblically by the bond-servant. A bond-servant was a slave who had been offered his freedom, but who, of his own volition, chose to remain a slave and serve his master faithfully. The master didn't force him to stay or to do his bidding, but it was the slave who chose joyfully and willingly to take on the role of servant. Our flesh doesn't like to hear that we "have to" do what God says. We don't naturally like anybody telling us that we "must" do something, let alone to deny ourselves and follow Christ in all areas. This is a high and intense calling, but it is our calling. We are called to be bond-servants who willingly surrender to Christ in order to accomplish His purposes and desires on the earth. We are to no longer concern ourselves with what we want but with what He wants. Our goals for life are not to be ours but His. Our objectives each day are not to be self-made but God-ordered. It is a completely different mindset than what is natural.

Consider the passage in Luke 17:7-10:

> "Which of you, having a slave plowing or tending sheep, will say to him when he has come in from the field, 'Come immediately and sit down to eat'? But will he not say to him, 'Prepare something for me to eat, and properly clothe yourself and serve me while I eat and drink; and afterward you may eat and drink'? He does not thank the slave because he did the things which were commanded, does he? So you too, when you do all the things which are commanded you, say, 'We are unworthy slaves; we have done only that which we ought to have done.'"

The thrust of this passage is that the will of the Master takes absolute precedence over the immediate needs and desires of the servant. He is in charge, and we are not. We do not deserve thanks for our service, for we are only doing what God has required of us in the first place. That is the conclusion of verse 10. It is not, "Wow, look at me and what I have done for God today. He must be impressed with me." Rather, it is that we are unworthy apart from Christ, and we do only what we are expected to do given our submissive role before Christ. Our calling as Christians is a submissive and subservient role before Christ. We are placed under His authority, for Christ is our head and our Master. He is Lord of our lives and Lord of the universe. This is not up for debate, nor is this optional in discipleship.

The revived person recognizes this and begins to model his life after Christ, Who Himself took on the form of a bond-servant. He left heaven with all of its wonderful rights and privileges and took on the form of a man. He was persecuted, He suffered, and He died on the cross for our sins. But He rose again, and God exalted Him above every name. This is why He is Lord. He first became the ultimate example of humility and servanthood, and now He will judge the world. We would do well to live in submission to the rightful Lord of our lives. If we want revival, we must take on the role of a bond-servant, bowing before the Master, seeking His kingdom first, and letting Him supply us with all of the rest of what we need.

Eternal Rewards

There is a disturbing lack of teaching in the church about eternal rewards for the believer. Perhaps that is because for many it does not touch a felt need and is irrelevant. This is not good. We need to be aware that how we live now has an effect upon our eternity in heaven. 2 Corinthians 5:10 says, "For we must all appear before the judgment seat of Christ, so that each one may be recompensed for his deeds in the body, according to what he has done, whether good or bad." All Christians will stand before Christ and give an account for how they used and invested what was given to them to advance the kingdom of God. Some have done well, while others have done poorly. But we must all give an account. This is why the New Testament is filled with exhortations that we not lose our reward and to be faithful so that we need not shrink away at Christ's coming in fear and shame (1 John 2:28). There will be great sorrow felt by those who have not been faithful and who come to realize what they are missing out on. But thanks be to God that heaven is still promised and available because of grace and faith in Christ. He will wipe away every tear, and He will welcome us home.

Many Christians haven't a clue about the subject of eternal rewards, and thus they have an additional temptation to live carnally. If it doesn't matter how they live, why should they bother to consecrate their lives to Christ? It does matter, and there will be some real disappointment for those who are not faithful. We are to seek to be first in the kingdom by being the servant of all in the here and now. This life fundamentally isn't about us. Why are we trying to sinfully get all we can out of eighty vain years when the opportunity for eternal honor and glory awaits?

1 Corinthians 3:10-15 says,

> "According to the grace of God which was given to me, like a wise master builder I laid a foundation, and another is building on it. But each man must be careful how he builds on it. For no man can lay a foundation other than the one which is laid, which is Jesus Christ. Now if any man builds on the foundation with gold, silver, precious stones, wood, hay, straw, each man's work will become evident; for the day will show it because it is to be revealed with fire, and the fire itself will test the quality of each man's work. If any man's work which he has built on it remains, he will receive a reward. If any man's work is burned up, he will suffer loss; but he himself will be saved, yet so as through fire."

What are we building on the foundation of Christ in our lives and in the lives of others? It is impossible to build anything that will endure this fiery test unless it has been built by Christ's power working through our lives. But are we taking advantage of it? Are we looking forward to judgment time before our Lord and Savior, Jesus Christ, the One who will judge the world? Are we living as one under authority, as one responsible as a caretaker, and as one who will have to give an account? We are under authority, we have a boss, and we will be held accountable for faithfulness or faithlessness.

A Kind and Faithful Master

Too many view the notion of being a servant of God as an experience that will make joy impossible. They view God as a cruel taskmaster, an unforgiving father figure, and a deity that enjoys our suffering and misery. God is none of those things, for in Him alone can true joy and pleasure be found (Psalm 16:11). Furthermore, in Jesus, we have a God Who understands our human condition and sympathizes with us (Hebrews 4:15-16). He has even promised to provide a way of escape when temptation comes (1 Corinthians 10:13). Our God is good, faithful, and true, full of mercy, gentleness, grace, and patience. It is a pleasure to serve such a God. God, after all, is the One Who told us that it is kindness that leads to repentance (Romans 2:4), not wrath. He teaches us through kindness, for even His discipline when we go off course is motivated by love.

Before we came to Christ, we were slaves of sin and unrighteousness, bound to do the bidding of the evil one. In such bondage, there is no freedom, no joy, and no hope, only the passing pleasures of sin that bring death, disappointment, and destruction. When we submit totally to God's control and will for our lives, we finally find true freedom, life, and joy because finally we are set free from the bondage of sin. Christ came to bring us life to the full, the abundant life (John 10:10), not to steal, kill, or destroy like the devil. When we finally understand just how good and kind God is, it only makes sense to want to follow Him, learn more about His ways, and obey His Word. Our view of God will either make us want to rebel against Him or submit to Him. A right view of God brings humility and a joyful submission and service to Him. This submission is a sure sign that a heart is being revived.

Section 2:

If My People Will "Pray…"

Chapter 4:
What is God's Design for Prayer?

*"Call to Me and I will answer you, and I will tell you great
and mighty things, which you do not know."*
Jeremiah 33:3

We have lost the supernatural in the American church. We think that we have things under control; thus, we see no reason that we absolutely must pray. We think we know far more than we actually do, when God wants to teach us things that we don't as of yet know. Most professing Christians do not pray even a minute or two a day, other than at mealtime, if even then. We have no conception of intercessory prayer, a prayer that pleads on behalf of a person, family, church, or nation. There is Biblical reason to believe that movements of God are preceded by the prayers of God's people (Nehemiah, David, Hannah, Christ, and the early church, to name a few) ascending to Him as incense. In fact, if professing Christians ever start getting together corporately to pray for change (and getting beyond praying simply for their aching back and safe travel home from the gathering), this would likely be the sign that revival is beginning. What joy it would bring to God's heart to hear God's people call upon His name!

There are few things that can compare to the spiritual joy that stems from being part of a group of committed Christians calling out to God for souls, for change, for renewal, and for growth. There is nothing inherently wrong with a prayer meeting that prays for needs within a church or for health problems or ministry directions. Those are wonderful, and may there be more of such meetings. However, our hearts should long for being part of a prayer group of other like minded men and women who have a burden for seeing change. Sadly, most are content with the status quo. They are involved with church activities, and there doesn't appear to be any urgency or desperation for souls or for the state of the church. Perhaps that is because they don't know how bad things actually are. Perhaps they need to be moved to brokenness. Perhaps they need to learn to call upon the Lord. **In the**

Bible, the way things got done was through a public reading of the Word, individual and corporate prayer, fasting, repentance, and worship. We try to get things done by introducing a recovery group, a therapy session, a new program, or by attending the latest conference of breakthrough ideas and strategies. As the culture changes, so we try to change. We are seriously off course. God's ways are the same today as they have always been. They are so simple, but so few actually abide by them. If only we could get some people to pray according to the Scripture and according to God's heart for revival, revival could be near.

Oh, that God would raise up more soul-winners! Of course, salvation is a gift of God, but we are called as witnesses (Acts 1:8). We should hope to have names of people whose salvation we can pray for. We should want to feed off the Spirit's leading through a gathering of believers as we call upon the Lord for change in this nation. If only we spent as much time investing vertically in prayer as we do horizontally in activity, change probably would have already occurred. If God leads us to be involved in some church activity, by all means we should do it. But it is too often the case that we are so preoccupied with the "work of the ministry" that we forget to pray, which is foundational to ministry and even part of the definition of it.

Jesus took only a few to disciple. He spread the church through them. If only God would prepare some hearts to be open to His leading, a prayer movement could begin and revival could start. But are we willing to tarry in prayer? How quickly would we expect an answer? Are we willing to pray for years with no results and keep doing it with increasing fervor? It seems that prayer is going out of fashion in the church because it does not often yield instant gratification, it is not user-friendly, and it does not entertain. Prayer often times is not a lot of fun. It is hard work, and it may move us to tears. Yet it must be done. In an age where gurus and entrepreneurs have church all figured out, prayer assumes helplessness and the surrender of control. Prayer is God's way. The answer for revival is so simple. If only God's people would approach God with clean hearts, broken spirits, and a trembling before His Word, then God could hear, answer, and heal.

The real disappointment is that we are prayer illiterate. The tendency is for the older generations to be fluent in prayer. They grew up praying in church, and it was normative to pray at least before meals and at bedtime. The sad thing is that the same churches where these folks grew up have now been transitioned into churches that have services in which no prayer is said whatsoever! Is prayer irrelevant? Is it too boring? For the unsaved, it absolutely is, but for the Christian? Where is the reliance on God, the desperate plea before the throne? The result of this is that the younger generations have almost no understanding of the role and purpose of prayer, and, in some cases, even how to pray. Perhaps this skill has not been passed on because the generation in between has gotten so carried away with programs and strategies. We need to turn this around, and we need to do prayer Biblically.

Re-examining Prayer

Prayer is one of those foundational Christian words that is so often used that it has almost no meaning to us. Here is a list of other words that we could substitute for the word "pray": implore, plead, beg, ask, entreat, request, call upon, urge, meditate, contemplate, hope, wish, yearn, and crave. How far short does our average prayer come from imploring, begging, entreating, contemplating, and craving? We have got to see that our need is great. Perhaps Satan is not using persecution on us because it might just wake us up. He has instead lulled us to sleep. If only we could learn to implore and beseech while a season of peace remains. May we not be so shallow that the only thing that will awaken us from our spiritual slumber is persecution. In the persecuted church, they do not have conferences and seminars on church growth techniques. They have prayer gatherings. If we want to be honest with God about our spirituality, we need only to look at our commitment to prayer. We may know a lot of Bible facts, but if our prayer lives are poor, we are off course in some major ways. May God teach us to pray, may He give us the desire to pray, and may He give us invested interests so that we are compelled to pray. May He push us out of our comfort zones so that we learn to pray. May He increase our faith so that we begin to believe that He can do the impossible. We need to be revived.

The Lord's Prayer

The Bible gives a very clear guideline for prayers that are effective. The disciples had been watching Jesus pray on a regular basis. Eventually they came to Him and asked, "Lord, teach us to pray." Is that where we are at? Do we want to be taught? Are we satisfied with our prayer lives? It is well worth our effort to examine what Jesus taught His disciples about prayer. They became experts in a few short years thanks to the Holy Spirit. Jesus took His novice pray-ers and gave them what we now know as the Lord's Prayer. If we wish to become better pray-ers, we need to learn what they learned. In Matthew 6:9-13, we read:

> "Pray, then, in this way: 'Our Father who is in heaven, Hallowed be Your name. Your kingdom come, Your will be done, On earth as it is in heaven. Give us this day our daily bread. And forgive us our debts, as we also have forgiven our debtors. And do not lead us into temptation, but deliver us from evil. [For Yours is the kingdom and the power and the glory forever. Amen.]'"

This prayer is given as a guideline for how we ought to pray as a general rule. Sometimes we will pray a quick thanksgiving prayer or ask God for help at a moment's notice. But generally, God is honored when we address Him with reverence and fear, praising His name and Who He is. Prayer ought to start out with praise whether in a group or all by ourselves. God needs to be exalted in our hearts even if we do not feel like it. It is a way for getting our hearts in the right posture and mindset. We are entering the presence of the God of the universe, the jealous God, and the God Who is a consuming fire. It is time for reverence and respect. We ought to address our prayers to the Father. The Son tells us to pray to the Father, and He now sits at the right hand of the Father interceding on our behalf. Our prayers are to go through Jesus as the Spirit enables to the Father. We then should pray for the kingdom in general to advance. We should pray for the church to influence culture, for souls to come to Christ, for God's ways to be reflected in government and in our sphere of influence. Our prayer should be that we will see heavenly ways replicated on earth.

    We are told to pray for daily bread to meet our needs for each day and to be able to have strength to serve the Lord. This helps us consecrate ourselves to Him, asking for opportunities to stand for righteousness and share our faith that day. It is a clear admission of our need for and dependence upon God.

We also should ask for forgiveness for any outstanding sin. If we regard sin in our hearts, God will not even hear our prayers. In addition, we must forgive those who have sinned against us, giving up any spirit of vengefulness, bitterness, and anger. Having set our focus on God and pursuing His purposes for our lives that day, we can expect Satan to come at us with everything he's got. Therefore, we are told to pray that God will keep us from falling into temptation and evil. We can pray that God will keep temptation from even coming our way. The final part of the prayer is not in all of the original manuscripts, but it sure can't hurt to praise God one final time for His power and glory.

The end of a prayer is prayed in the name of Jesus, for only through Him do we have the right to go to the Father. John 16:23 says, "In that day you will not question Me about anything. Truly, truly, I say to you, if you ask the Father for anything in My name, He will give it to you." Prayer is to the Father in the name of Jesus, without Whom we cannot access the presence and throne of God. Since, however, we have Jesus in our hearts, we can approach the throne of grace boldly to receive help in time of need (Hebrews 4:16). The prayer is closed with "Amen," meaning "so be it," "I agree," or "may it be done."

The Lord's Prayer is our model for prayer. It is a basic outline, but it can be very helpful for organizing our prayer lives and for guiding a corporate prayer meeting.

Prerequisites for Answered Prayer

There are a lot of discouraged pray-ers out there. Perhaps that is because God has not answered because we have not prayed in a way that aligns with His design for prayer. God's Word gives us some clear guidelines for how we must pray if we want to see answers to our prayers. Here are five characteristics of effective prayers:

1. Faith

Mark 11:22-24 says,

"And Jesus answered saying to them, 'Have faith in God. Truly I say to you, whoever says to this mountain, "Be taken up and cast into the sea," and does not doubt in his heart, but believes that what he says is going to happen, it will be granted him. Therefore I say to you, all things for which you pray and ask, believe that you have received them, and they will be granted you.'"

The principle here is that we must have faith that we have received what we have asked of God in order to receive it. If we believe that we are praying according to God's will, we ought to pray boldly and in faith. We cannot doubt the will of God and expect answers to prayer. God doesn't promise to answer the prayers of a double-minded man waffling between faith and doubt (James 1:7-8).

2. Persistence

Luke 11:5-10 says,

"Then He said to them, 'Suppose one of you has a friend, and goes to him at midnight and says to him, "Friend, lend me three loaves; for a friend of mine has come to me from a journey, and I have nothing to set before him"; and from inside he answers and says, "Do not bother me; the door has already been shut and my children and I are in bed; I cannot get up and give you anything." I tell you, even though he will not get up and give him anything because he is his friend, yet because of his persistence he will get up and give him as much as he needs. So I say to you, ask, and it will be given to you; seek, and you will find; knock, and it will be opened to you. For everyone who asks, receives; and he who seeks, finds; and to him who knocks, it will be opened.'"

The clear lesson in this story is that God honors persistence in prayer. God doesn't always give us what we ask for right away. Sometimes He tests our faith by allowing us to have to continually and consistently seek God in prayer. Persistence demonstrates faith. If we want to see answers to our prayers, we need to tarry in prayer, not just one time, but over and over again, not losing heart all the while. Programs and quick fixes seem a lot more palatable, especially to an uncommitted church attendee. But revival can only happen God's way, and tarrying in prayer is His way.

3. Without Ceasing

1 Thessalonians 5:17 gives us another qualification for answered prayer. It says that we must "pray without ceasing." This could mean several things. It clearly echoes the fact that we must be persistent and persevering in our praying. However, as an individual, it is impossible to literally get into a prayer closet and never get out. That is practically not a good application of the passage. This could be rationalized away by saying that we should maintain an attitude of prayerfulness throughout the day as we consider all that happens in light of what the Lord would have us do. But if we consider that the command is written not to an individual but to a church as a whole, the exhortation could be applied to the community of faith. The church should be praying unceasingly. Many churches have a prayer room or prayer tower where people sign up to intercede for an hour each day. This is a literal application of the command. We sure can't argue against prayer around the clock. However, without getting bent out of shape over the "letter of the law," we would do well to apply the heart of the exhortation, which is to be praying regularly, frequently, often, and without ceasing. The idea is that prayer is important, so we should do it a lot, do it regularly, do it often, and while we are at it, keep doing it. The church must be marked by prayer, for it is a house of prayer. Practically, we should be looking to find ways to grow in our prayer lives so as to fulfill the spirit of the command and seek to please the heart of God. As both individuals and churches, the goal for prayer has been set high because God values its importance just as highly.

4. Righteousness

James 5:16, probably the most often quoted verse on prayer, gives us a rule about prayer that we often take for granted. It says, "The effective prayer of a righteous man can accomplish much." The principle which this passage exposes is that the church's prayer, as well as the individual's, is hindered by the presence of unconfessed sin. This idea is illustrated with a practical example in 1 Peter 3:7 which says, "You husbands in the same way, live with your wives in an understanding way, as with someone weaker, since she is a woman; and show her honor as a fellow heir of the grace of life, so that your prayers will not be hindered." If husbands are not treating their wives as God has commanded, they can expect not to receive answers to their prayers. In fact, praying might be difficult to begin with. As a church, do we want to see answered prayer? Are we tired of feeling like our prayers get "returned to sender"? We must examine our hearts and lives, and we must confess any outstanding sin to God and to those we have sinned against. God promises to forgive us, and we can go back to enjoying the promise and blessing of answered prayer.

5. According to God's Will

1 John 5:14-15 reminds us that we must pray according to His will if we want to see our prayers answered. It says, "And this is the confidence that we have before Him, that, if we ask anything according to His will, He hears us. And if we know that He hears us in whatever we ask, we know that we have the requests which we have asked from Him." To ask according to His will means that we are praying in accordance with what God wants done. This is no problem if we are abiding in Christ, for then He will guide us into what we ought to pray. The more we study God's Word, the better we will know what to pray for. For example, God wants people to come to Him, so we should pray for that. God wants us to be sanctified, so we should pray for that. God wants to lead His people and give them wisdom, so we should pray accordingly. As we do so with clean hearts and in perseverance, we should expect God to answer in His perfect wisdom and according to His sovereign timetable. We never manipulate God in prayer, but rather we get to align ourselves with His will and be part of His plan and work on the earth.

The Spirit's Intercession

The Biblical road to revival is no simple quick fix or three-steps-to-success formula. Prayer is a spiritual labor by faith and through Christ's power. Romans 8:26-27 says,

"In the same way the Spirit also helps our weakness; for we do not know how to pray as we should, but the Spirit Himself intercedes for us with groanings too deep for words; and He who searches the hearts knows what the mind of the Spirit is, because He intercedes for the saints according to the will of God."

We must acknowledge before God that we are, left to ourselves, horrible pray-ers. We don't know what we should say or pray. We don't know how to ascertain the mind of God. We don't know how to pray properly, and we don't know how to pray according to the will of God. That is the truth of the Romans passage. We can't do it alone. The Spirit will help us in our weakness and intercede for us so that we can pray properly to the Father and according to His will. Praise God for His wonderful and perfect grace! He will do what we cannot.

Prayer that is led and empowered by the Spirit of God is a major key that turns the lock of revival. In fact, in revival, once hearts are broken by the Word to be open to God (which may itself have been rooted in the prayers of others), prayer to God for repentance and change is the natural consequence. The question remains for us: will we be committed to praying for revival in our own hearts which will lead to evangelization of the lost?

Chapter 5:
Commit to Corporate and Individual Prayer

"And He said to them, 'It is written, "MY HOUSE SHALL BE CALLED A HOUSE OF PRAYER."'"
Matthew 21:13

Acts 2:42 tells us that the early church was devoted to prayer. Many times in the epistles we see how Paul poured out his heart in prayer for those to whom he had preached the gospel. Prayer is a major theme throughout the New Testament. The curious thing about talking to the church about prayer is that no one will argue about the importance of prayer. However, if we want to see revival, we are not doing what we ought to be doing in the area of prayer. It is much more common to view the church as a fishing net, a boring ritualistic environment, or a house of entertainment than it is to see it as a house of prayer. If we are honest with ourselves, picturing the church as a house of prayer is not the first thing that comes to mind when we think about the church. In fact, it is far down the list. It ought to be right near the top, for it is how Jesus viewed the assembling of the saints (Matthew 21:13). Committing to corporate and individual prayer is crucial in order to see the church revived and the lost saved.

The Absolute Necessity of Prayer

We know that Jesus prayed all the time, which tells us that He must have seen the absolute importance of prayer to His life and ministry, even though He was God in the flesh. If Jesus needed to pray, we must really need to pray. The following gives several reasons why Jesus prayed:

1. Because He Needed to.

Luke 5:15-16 says, "But the news about Him was spreading even farther, and large crowds were gathering to hear Him and to be healed of their sicknesses. But Jesus Himself would often slip away to the wilderness and pray." From a human perspective, He had all kinds of ministry He could be doing. If He were a pastor, His church would have been bursting at the seams. Would we slip away to take time to pray if we had people thronging to our churches looking to us for help and counsel? This is not our natural reaction, but it is what Jesus did often. He would slip away to the wilderness and find a quiet place to pray. Why would He do this? He was God in human flesh, and He showed us what we need to do at all times, even when there are all kinds of opportunities for ministry. His flesh was weak just as ours is, and He knew that if He was going to keep from temptation and stay the course to accomplish that for which He had come, He had better pray. Yet too often we think that we are strong enough to skip the praying. We are wrong. We will fall for temptation, become prideful, grow tired, become mixed up in our priorities, and lose sight of what God is doing. These were good times of ministry for Jesus from a perspective of numbers and popularity. Yet for Jesus that was all the more reason to pray. We have got to slip away to a quiet place and pray. For Jesus, prayer in a quiet place was absolutely essential. Jesus prayed because He needed to. How much more do we need to be relying upon God and seeking Him in prayer?

2. To Stay Focused on His Mission

In Mark 1:33-38 we read,

"And the whole city had gathered at the door. And He healed many who were ill with various diseases, and cast out many demons; and He was not permitting the demons to speak, because they knew who He was. In the early morning, while it was still dark, Jesus got up, left the house, and went away to a secluded place, and was praying there. Simon and his companions searched for Him; they found Him, and said to Him, 'Everyone is looking for You.' He said to them, 'Let us go somewhere else to the towns nearby, so that I may preach there also; for that is what I came for.'"

From our perspective, Jesus had another golden ministry opportunity here, yet He left the crowd and went into other towns to proclaim the advent of the kingdom. He prayed to keep His vision clear, His mission central, and His priorities in balance. He wanted to stay on track with where the Father was leading Him. A key part in revival is that we each do what God has given us to do and go where He has led us to go. Each of us must do our part of the work and carry our portion of the burden. Prayer will give us the direction and focus to do the tasks that God would have us do in the short duration of our lives on this earth. God doesn't always lead to the crowds. Sometimes He leads us to quiet or to trials. The key is that we go where He is leading so that we stay focused on His mission for us.

3. To Make Crucial Decisions

The point at which Jesus chose His twelve disciples was a crucial point in His ministry. There are times in ministry, in life, or in a church's history which could be described as major ministry moments or crucial decision-making instances. Jesus had one such instance here. It shouldn't come as a surprise what He did—He prayed. Luke 6:12-13 says, "It was at this time that He went off to the mountain to pray, and He spent the whole night in prayer to God. And when day came, He called His disciples to Him and chose twelve of them, whom He also named as apostles." When the Scripture says "at this time," it is referring to a time in Jesus' life when the Pharisees and religious leaders were filled with rage at Jesus. Jesus left them, knowing that they were plotting to harm Him. He decided to take a prayer retreat overnight. He prayed all night and then chose His disciples.

In the face of difficulty and enemies, we must pray. When we need direction, peace, and a clear mind, prayer is the remedy. Jesus relied upon the Father's direction and the Spirit's leading, knowing the next day He would be selecting those who would change the history of the world. If we are in a difficult spot, we should pray as our first and immediate reaction. Some churches do this, and praise God for that. However, most get the key thinkers behind closed doors and use their brain power to devise a way out. We do not need a human think tank. We need God. Jesus prayed all night in order to be able to sense God's leading in choosing His disciples. How much do we pray when we have significant decisions to make? For revival to occur, our reaction to hardship and in key decisions must be prayer.

4. To Resist Temptation

In Matthew 26, we are given an account of Jesus and the disciples in the Garden of Gethsemane. In verse 41, Jesus told the disciples, "Keep watching and praying that you may not enter into temptation; the spirit is willing, but the flesh is weak." Jesus knew that He had to stay up all night and pray so that He would be ready for what was about to happen and so that He would not fall into temptation before that time. Jesus needed to pray to resist temptation. If Jesus needed to pray to have strength to resist Satan, how much more must we need to pray to overcome and resist temptation? Prayer is not just a nice idea, a Christian discipline, and something church people do. It is a way of life and an absolute necessity for living as Christ would have us.

Christians give in to temptation left and right in the western church. Sins are mistakes rather than abominations. Jesus told us in the Lord's Prayer to regularly pray that we would be delivered from evil and kept from temptation. Perhaps we can learn to pray offensively against Satan's attacks rather than for comfort and resolution after the flaming missile has done its damage. In times of revival, Satan's work is impeded because of prayer.

5. For Strength

In Mark 6:45-47 says, "Immediately Jesus made His disciples get into the boat and go ahead of Him to the other side to Bethsaida, while He Himself was sending the crowd away. After bidding them farewell, He left for the mountain to pray." Jesus just spent a long day ministering to the crowds. His disciples got in the boat to go home. He headed for the mountain to pray. At evening, He walked to them on the water and met up with them. But before He met up with them, He took precious time to reenergize in the Lord in prayer and to get focused once again. When we are fatigued after a long day and from discipling others or serving God in some way, we need to pray for wisdom and protection. We need to pray that Satan will not steal the seeds that have been planted. Christ had a long day of work, but He didn't wait to pray. Perhaps it is the fact that prayer tends to lessen once spiritual advancements are made which contributes to the fact that revival is rarely sustained for any length of time. Once a key victory is won, it is easy to celebrate and stop going on the offensive. We can never become complacent or careless until Christ comes. We must keep fighting and tarrying in prayer.

6. As an Essential Component of Effective Ministry

Jesus also took time to pray in ministry settings. After others were baptized and He Himself was baptized, He prayed. Luke 3:21 says,

> "Now when all the people were baptized, Jesus was also baptized, and while He was praying, heaven was opened and the Holy Spirit descended upon Him in bodily form like a dove, and a voice came out of heaven, 'You are My beloved Son, in You I am well-pleased.'"

Obviously God was pleased by Jesus being baptized, but is it possible that He was additionally pleased by Jesus' obedience to pray? It was while He was praying that the Spirit descended and the voice from heaven spoke. Even at His own baptism, He prayed. Do we pray even in the regular tasks of ministry and life? God is honored by that. In fact, it is essential for our well-being and spiritual growth. A mark of revival is that every activity and ministry is bathed in prayer that and prayer is a component of all events and activities. No decision or activity is too trivial that it cannot be prayed for. In revival, prayer becomes an integral part of the spiritual equation. Yet so often this is not the case.

7. To Endure Hardship

Matthew 4:1-11 records the temptation of Jesus by the devil. Jesus fasted for forty days, obviously praying to God throughout to ready Himself for ministry. When He returned from successfully resisting temptation, He began His ministry. What is the lesson for us here? When God leads us into wilderness times in life and ministry, prayer becomes all the more important. Just as good times can corrupt our hearts with pride, difficult times can deceive our hearts with doubt and despair. In times of temptation and struggle, we must commit to prayer. Jesus needed to pray in order to be able to resist temptation and be sustained in His wilderness experience. In weakness, He was strong by faith in God's sustenance. If Jesus needed prayer in His trial, all the more must we.

There are times in life that are so hard that it is difficult to even concentrate enough to pray. Perhaps in those times we can meditate upon a single Scripture, or we might try writing out a prayer. Writing out prayers can serve to keep our minds focused and to organize our thoughts and feelings before God. We cannot afford to skip praying when difficulty and disaster lurk all around us.

Jesus needed to pray, and prayer was an integral part to His life on earth. In tough times and in good times, prayer was His way. It kept Him from sin and kept His eyes on the Father. If Jesus needed to pray, how much more must we need to pray. **The conclusion must be this: revival cannot and does not exist apart from prayer.**

Practical Helps for the Individual

1. Isolate

It is probably best to set a regular time for prayer each day, preferably before the daily grind. Yet this is not a Biblical requirement, and it should not become legalistic. We already saw how Jesus prayed at all different hours of the day, depending upon the circumstances. David also prayed at nearly every time throughout the day. The important thing is that prayer happens. The goal is that we isolate ourselves from the daily grind and routine and get to a place of quiet. There we can concentrate and let go of life's distractions so we can listen to what the Lord wants to show us in our hearts and in our lives according to His Word. As it says in Matthew 6:6, "But you, when you pray, go into your inner room, close your door and pray to your Father who is in secret, and your Father who sees what is done in secret will reward you." It needs to be just God and us and nothing else. Someone will argue that they don't have time for this. The fact is that we have time for what we think is important. Those who value prayer as absolutely essential like Jesus did will make time no matter what. While the baby naps, while on lunch break, or before the family awakens could all be ways to find a few precious moments to be with our Lord. **Jesus was the expert at finding inconvenient times to pray.** In fact, more often than not prayer is inconvenient. Yet, as Jesus did, the key is that we make time and pray.

2. Meditate

Meditation is a lost art today. It is also a confused art. It is not an emptying of the brain to try to reach some spiritual reality. It is not some mystical experience about becoming one with God and hearing some actual voice or feeling some warm, loving feeling. It is a filling of the mind with God's Word, God's character, and God's works. Hence we should take a Bible with us when we are praying. It might be helpful to read some of God's Word first before we pray so that our prayer will be in response to what we have gleaned from the Scripture. We might also pray before we even read the Word that God will teach us and lead us through His Word. Perhaps we might pick a particular book of the Bible and read meditatively through a chapter or section until God draws our attention to a convicting truth or an enlightening thought. If we come across something we don't understand, we might use that as an opportunity to dig deeper into our study. The more we study and understand Scripture, the better and more accurately we will be able to pray. Meditation is not about getting some new revelation from the Lord, for the canon of Scripture is complete. In God's Word, we have all that we need for life and godliness (2 Peter 1:3). Rather, we meditate to reflect upon His truths and on His working in our lives. We are to try to determine by the Spirit's leading what God would have us change. We are to seek to determine what He would have us become or do.

How often should we meditate? Joshua 1:8 says,

> "This book of the law shall not depart from your mouth, but you shall meditate on it day and night, so that you may be careful to do according to all that is written in it; for then you will make your way prosperous, and then you will have success."

Day and night is an awfully long time to meditate, but it is God's design. Psalm 1:2 says of the righteous man, "But his delight is in the law of the LORD, And in His law he meditates day and night." There ought never to be a moment when we are conscious that we are not aware of God and His bearing on our lives. We may not always be meditating consciously upon God, but we should never be cognizant that we are ignoring God. If we are, we need to get back to a quiet place and meditate. We are to meditate on God's precepts, wonders, ways, statutes, and works. There is never going to be a lack of wonder about God to think upon. There is no way that we can be what God wants and live as He desires if we are not reflecting throughout the day upon His truths. This gives the Holy Spirit opportunity to transform our minds according to God's Word. We have no problem reflecting and even dreaming about a movie we saw or rehearsing a song we heard on the radio over and over in our heads. Yet, too often, we do not think about God and what He is doing and desiring according to His Word. This is a shame, and it ought to expose to us what we value and where our hearts are. We need to get back to the basics and repent. Do we want to prosper in our spiritual growth and effectiveness? Do we want to be revived? We had better meditate on God's Word. There is no way that we can lay aside the weights and entanglements of sin in order to fix our eyes upon Christ unless we meditate upon God's Word. It must saturate our minds and hearts. God's Word is what our minds should be focused on. The Spirit will then lead us to apply the truth to various areas of life.

3. Evaluate

There comes a time in our prayer lives that we need to ask God to search our hearts. Psalm 139:23-24 says, "Search me, O God, and know my heart; Try me and know my anxious thoughts; And see if there be any hurtful way in me, And lead me in the everlasting way." If we have any unconfessed sin, God will put that at the forefront of our minds to deal with. He wants us to deal with our outstanding sin issues right away before He will reveal anything else to us. If there are any underlying sin issues that we may not be aware of, we need to ask God to show them to us. We are works in progress, and we have sin patterns of which we are as of yet unaware. There are weak areas that God wants to strengthen.

We must let Him speak to us through His Word to show us where He wants us to change.

4. Initiate

There is no point in taking all of the time to pray, meditate, and evaluate and then not bothering to put into practice what the Lord has put His finger on. James 1:22-25 says,

> "But prove yourselves doers of the word, and not merely hearers who delude themselves. For if anyone is a hearer of the word and not a doer, he is like a man who looks at his natural face in a mirror; for once he has looked at himself and gone away, he has immediately forgotten what kind of person he was. But one who looks intently at the perfect law, the law of liberty, and abides by it, not having become a forgetful hearer but an effectual doer, this man will be blessed in what he does."

We look in a mirror and get bent out of shape over a zit, peeling skin, broccoli between the teeth, or any other physical mar, spot, wrinkle, or stain. In nearly every case, we will act immediately to deal with such a problem. We ought to be as troubled by any sin issue that God has identified. It is easy to forget what God has taught us, and so we must make a point of putting God's Word into practice. It is vain, pointless, and just plain dumb to take all of the time and energy to hear from God and then not do what He says. We must be doers of the Word and not hearers only. Few Christians do what James says in abiding in Christ and His Word by keeping short accounts with God. This is why many lead fruitless lives, get deceived, and live in confusion and double-mindedness. Upon the conviction and the leading of God, we ought to act immediately to repent and obey.

Practical Helps for the Local Church

The book of Acts is replete with examples of corporate prayer in the early church from which we have a lot to learn. Here is a brief list of examples:

- Acts 1:13-15 says, "When they had entered the city, they went up to the upper room where they were staying; that is, Peter and John and James and Andrew, Philip and Thomas, Bartholomew and Matthew, James the son of Alphaeus, and Simon the Zealot, and Judas the son of James. These all with one mind were continually devoting themselves to prayer, along with the women, and Mary the mother of Jesus, and with His brothers." In verse 15 we read that there were 120 followers of Christ there, not just the 11 disciples.
- Peter and John returned to their companions after being threatened by the Jewish leaders, and they prayed. Acts 4:31 records the result, saying, "And when they had prayed, the place where they had gathered together was shaken, and they were all filled with the Holy Spirit and began to speak the word of God with boldness."
- In Acts 13:1-3, we read, "Now there were at Antioch, in the church that was there, prophets and teachers: Barnabas, and Simeon who was called Niger, and Lucius of Cyrene, and Manaen who had been brought up with Herod the tetrarch, and Saul. While they were ministering to the Lord and fasting, the Holy Spirit said, 'Set apart for Me Barnabas and Saul for the work to which I have called them.' After the Holy Spirit chose Paul and Barnabas to go out as missionaries, the church prayed for them." The entire church here is credited as praying for Paul and Barnabas before they go out as missionaries.
- Acts 16:25-26 says, "But about midnight Paul and Silas were praying and singing hymns of praise to God, and the prisoners were listening to them; and suddenly there came a great earthquake, so that the foundations of the prison house were shaken; and immediately all the doors were opened and everyone's chains were unfastened." Paul and Silas together took advantage of their time in prison to pray and worship God.
- Acts 20:36 says, "When he had said these things, he knelt down and prayed with them all." Paul and the elders and maybe some of the church all prayed together to bid him farewell.
- Acts 21:5 says, "When our days there were ended, we left and started on our journey, while they all, with wives and children,

escorted us until we were out of the city. After kneeling down on the beach and praying, we said farewell to one another." In this account, men, women and children all prayed together for the apostles.

There is no question whatsoever that praying together was a normative experience of the church. All members took part, including men, women, and children. There were elders and missionaries and people from all walks of life. As children become able, they need to be included as much as possible in church functions, especially prayer. The beauty of prayer is that all believers are alike before God in their right through Christ to approach God in prayer. There is not male and female, Jew or Gentile, slave or free, for all are one in Christ (Galatians 3:28). Christ is impartial, and prayer unifies. One of the early church's main functions was a devotion to prayer. Only remnants of such a picture remain in today's church in America.

So what must we do? The message and challenge is that we do something to put the priority of prayer on people's radar screen of what is important, even essential, in life. We want to encourage them to pray in their small groups and at their Bible studies and in their homes and as individuals. **But the challenge is to develop a mentality that church is a community, and prayer is something that we do together.** One of the best ways to build community is by doing ministry together. Prayer happens to be a very fundamental God-given way that we can love one another and build community. In order to make prayer a community activity, church leaders ought to pray as God leads with those in the church community even as they come into church or before they leave. Those younger in the Lord need to see those deeper in the Lord pray. They need to see and hear and perceive spiritually what a Spirit-led prayer is all about. Perhaps pastors could do a series on the great prayers in the Bible. Churches should set a time each week to gather corporately and pray. Some churches might opt to have people sign up to pray for a particular time slot or for a particular number of needs. One small church has an intercessory prayer room. Requests from all over the country are sent there, and little cards are sent out through the mail telling those who needed the prayer that they are being prayed for along with a relevant Scripture. It is important that people in the church are aware of needs. It is impossible to pray for one another if information does not get shared. Some means of communication is necessary so that requests are known. These are all ways to raise awareness of the need and value of prayer in the corporate body.

Life and church and ministry must be bathed in the prayers of God's people. God will hear and listen if we pray as we ought. Church leaders are responsible for seeing that their churches are praying churches. When will we realize that a spiritual battle must be fought on spiritual terms? It would be wiser from a Biblical standpoint to judge the health of a church based upon its commitment to prayer rather than upon the size of its building or the number of people who attend on a Sunday. If we are at all interested in revival, we will not see it unless we as a church learn to make prayer a priority.

A word to ministry leaders, particularly pastors and elders

It is tempting to think that the role of an elder is simply to govern the business affairs of the church, to solve difficult conflicts and disputes, and to teach and preach the Word of God. Certainly all of those ministries are important, but we must be mindful of God's Word. Acts 6:3-5 says, "Therefore, brethren, select from among you seven men of good reputation, full of the Spirit and of wisdom, whom we may put in charge of this task. But we will devote ourselves to prayer and to the ministry of the word." Seven men were chosen to help minister to the widows' needs. This freed up the elders to do more study of the Word and to pray. The ministry of the Word is extremely important, requiring a lot of study and time. Counseling, preaching, teaching, and writing all fall under the category of the ministry of the Word. But we cannot gloss over the fact that the apostles were devoting themselves also to prayer. It is the responsibility of church leaders to set the example and encourage prayer in their church. If they do not, no matter how good their study, they may miss some things that the Spirit would have them do and say. Prayer is absolutely essential to ministry and to the health of the corporate body of Christ. It is such a basic, simple truth, but until it is done, it must be repeatedly emphasized.

If we want to advance a spiritual kingdom, prayer is a spiritual means which the Spirit will gladly empower to spur revival. Prayer is more than a religious exercise and formality. It is a lifestyle, a posture, a begging, and a means to move mountains. It is the means to awaken hearts unto revival.

Section 3:

If My People Will "Seek My Face…"

Chapter 6:
What Does It Mean to Seek God's Face?

*"Brethren, do not be children in your thinking;
yet in evil be infants, but in your thinking be mature."
1 Corinthians 14:20*

Seeking God's face is probably the most misunderstood of all of the elements in 2 Chronicles 7:14. It is terminology that we use in singing and occasionally in praying, yet few of us really know what we are asking or singing. It is absolutely important that we know what the Bible is saying so that we don't devise our own incorrect interpretations. Psalm 27:8 says, "When You said, 'Seek My face,' my heart said to You, 'Your face, O LORD, I shall seek.'" Psalm 105:4 says, "Seek the LORD and His strength; Seek His face continually." In 1 Chronicles 16:11, this command is repeated: "Seek the LORD and His strength; Seek His face continually." God commands us to seek His face, and He expects that we are doing it continually. Thus, we had better be certain that we know what God intends by commanding us to seek His face, or we will be violating His commands continually. What is for sure is that it doesn't mean trying to see God's actual face unless we wish to die. Exodus 33:20 says, "But He said, 'You cannot see My face, for no man can see Me and live!'"

The word for "face" that is used in 2 Chronicles 7:14 and the one of primary usage in the Old Testament is *paneh*. *Paneh* means "the face as the part that turns." Its root word literally means "to turn." What exactly is it that is turning and why are we to seek its turning? The Bible says that God hides His face. Psalm 13:1 says, "How long, O LORD? Will You forget me forever? How long will You hide Your face from me?" Micah 3:4 says, "Then they will cry out to the LORD, But He will not answer them. Instead, He will hide His face from them at that time Because they have practiced evil deeds." When there is evil going on and sin being overlooked, God will hide His face. Here He is refraining from intervening, protecting, and blessing. When God hides

His face, we can expect to feel forgotten and experience sorrow. In addition to hiding His face, the Bible teaches that God turns His face away and pours out judgment, wrath, and destruction against a person or nation. Psalm 34:15-16 says, "The eyes of the LORD are toward the righteous And His ears are open to their cry. The face of the LORD is against evildoers, To cut off the memory of them from the earth." In Jeremiah 44:11 God says, "Therefore thus says the LORD of hosts, the God of Israel, 'Behold, I am going to set My face against you for woe, even to cut off all Judah.'" The Biblical consequences of God setting His face against are judgment and wrath. Scripture also teaches that God sets His face to shine upon us. Psalm 31:16 says, "Make Your face to shine upon Your servant; Save me in Your lovingkindness." When God sets His face toward us, we can expect blessing, help, and spiritual prosperity.

We Must Seek His Blessing

So it becomes clear that we should want to have God shine His face upon us. We don't want Him to hide His face, and we certainly don't want Him to turn His face against us. What is turning, then, is God's blessing. If we sin, He will hide His face, and for those who store up His wrath, He will turn His face against. We want His face to be for us, shining down upon us in blessing and favor. This really matters. How can we do anything of value for the kingdom if God's blessing and favor do not rest upon us? We have no chance to succeed. We must come to God desiring His favor and blessing, for without that we are powerless, empty, and helpless.

Genesis 39:21 says, "But the LORD was with Joseph and extended kindness to him, and gave him favor in the sight of the chief jailer." Joseph had a tough life, but God had a purpose for him. Joseph walked rightly before God, and God gave him His favor. Would Joseph have risen to second in command in Egypt without God's favor? Would he have ever gotten out of prison? Joseph needed God's favor, and so do we. We must seek it. As 2 Chronicles 16:9 says, "For the eyes of the LORD move to and fro throughout the earth that He may strongly support those whose heart is completely His." God is seeking worshippers, and He is looking for those who are seeking His face. We need His favor, and so we desperately ought to crave His support. We should want Him to turn His face of blessing upon us and to shine His face upon us. The Lord has told us to seek His face if we want to see revival. We must clearly acknowledge that we need His face by asking for His grace, blessing, and the pouring out of His Spirit to move in our hearts. This is something we ought to include in our individual and corporate times of prayer. We ought to pray that God will shine His face upon us. On a chilly fall day it feels good, healthy, fulfilling, and invigorating to feel the sun pop out from behind a cloud and shine down upon us. Literally the temperature can change ten to twenty degrees in mere instants. May God shine down upon us and elevate our spiritual temperature for desiring Him and for revival. The shining of His face upon us can make or break our hopes for revival.

We Must Seek According to Knowledge

Yet there is more to seeking God's face than just praying for His blessing. It is reasonable to suppose that, in 2 Chronicles 7:14, God separated His command to pray and His command to seek His face for a reason. For prayer to be powerful and effective, it must be according to truth. Likewise, a more adequate seeking of God's face requires a more adequate understanding of God Himself. Thus, seeking God's face involves getting increased knowledge of God so that we can more effectively and fully pray to Him, worship Him, and enjoy Him.

1 Corinthians 13:12 says, "For now we see in a mirror dimly, but then face to face; now I know in part, but then I will know fully just as I also have been fully known." When we get to heaven, we will see Jesus face to face. Our Lord knows us fully now, through and through without any lack of understanding or insight. We do not know Him even remotely close to fully. But when we see Him face to face, then we will know Him fully just as He knows us fully now. Thus, the better we know God, the more we grow into His likeness and the more we rightly seek His face. **It is via the knowledge of God, which only the Holy Spirit can supply through God's Word, that we seek God's face.**

2 Corinthians 3:18 says, "But we all, with unveiled face, beholding as in a mirror the glory of the Lord, are being transformed into the same image from glory to glory, just as from the Lord, the Spirit." Our spirits

and minds are not veiled to being able to relate to God and perceive His wonder and glory, for we are new creations in Christ. We are to be seeing God's glory and being transformed accordingly. When we look into a mirror of our hearts and souls, we are to see a reflection of the character and attributes of God. We are to see Christ Himself living within us. As 2 Corinthians 4:6 says, "For God, who said, 'Light shall shine out of darkness,' is the One who has shone in our hearts to give the Light of the knowledge of the glory of God in the face of Christ." So how do we more adequately see Christ in the spiritual mirror of our hearts? We see Him more adequately as He gives us the knowledge of the glory of God. It is through knowledge of our Savior and Lord that we are able to "see" His face more clearly. If we are to seek God's face, we must seek the knowledge and wisdom of God. Those who worship God must worship not just in spirit but also in truth (John 4:24). We can not become mature in our worship if we do not have truth. We ought not to worship in childish ways, but we ought to put childish ways behind us and worship like mature men and women of God.

1 John 4:7-8 says, "Beloved, let us love one another, for love is from God; and everyone who loves is born of God and knows God. The one who does not love does not know God, for God is love." We all want to love God better and more fully. He already loves us completely and entirely; He cannot love us more. We, however, can love Him more as our understanding of Him increases. Our love of God ought to be increasing as we see Christ's reflection in our hearts more and more clearly. Without the knowledge of God, there is no love of God. With a little knowledge of God, there can be a little love of God. It can be fully sincere love, but it is still small. It may be of tremendous quality, but it still is of a diminutive quantity. As knowledge increases, so too can our love for God. To see Him in a new light, to appreciate a newly understood attribute, to see God as He really is as beyond understanding, and to recognize His holiness all help us to love God more and more according to truth. Thus we become better worshippers of God as well. If we really want to love God, we must grow in our knowledge of Him through His Word. As we seek God's face, we must seek Him according to knowledge.

Seeking God's Face Is Crucial to Revival

A revived life is one which is revived according to knowledge. This person is a growing worshipper of God in both spirit and in truth. To seek God's face, then, we must seek His blessing according to the knowledge of His character. **Maturity in our knowledge and understanding of Christ is essential to our being revived.** Some people have been Christians for decades and still are babies in their thinking. No longer can we afford to deceive ourselves about the importance of knowing God and His Word. Study cannot be a bad or uncomfortable word within the church. It is hard work and not always fun, but it is the command of God. May He teach us to love His Word so that it is our greatest joy and not drudgery in any way. Let us begin now to seek His face so that we need not be ashamed at His coming. May we grow to the fullness of the measure and stature that is found in Christ, and may we be disciples who know the full counsel of God and who can divide it accurately. If we wish to experience revival at all, we must love and study the Word of God.

Chapter 7:
Develop a Mature Biblical Framework of Knowledge

"But speaking the truth in love, we are to grow up in all aspects into Him who is the head, even Christ."
Ephesians 4:15

Francis Schaeffer described a belief in the inerrant, infallible, and inspired Word of God as the watershed issue for the church in America. Yet, a few decades later, a more subtle deception has come into play. It is not so much a struggle with liberalism and conservatism over the inerrancy of God's Word; rather, it is a struggle within the ranks of those who would call themselves committed to the authority of God's Word. **There is the temptation and trend not to teach the full counsel of God.** Theology is regarded as irrelevant to the every day needs felt by church attendees and "seekers." In fact, theology is minimized, and for many people it is of no interest whatsoever. The great and core doctrines of the faith are unknown to many Christians today. They have all the tools to get as much as they can out of this life, but they do not know doctrine. Nor are they as concerned as they ought to be about the life to come. Too many churches never give their people the opportunity to grow to a spiritual maturity in their knowledge of Christ because they never teach the difficult elements of Scripture, let alone the foundational doctrinal truths that are essential to distinguishing Christianity from other world religions. They don't even expect their people to know where the books of the Bible are, let alone where to find a verse when they need one. This trend away from teaching the full counsel of God and from arming God's people with truth is frightening. In a day and age where Bibles are in the hand of nearly every man, woman, and child, Bible illiteracy and poor theology reign supreme. This is a disaster.

Paul says in 1 Corinthians 3:1-3, "And I, brethren, could not speak to you as to spiritual men, but as to men of flesh, as to infants in Christ. I gave you milk to drink, not solid food; for you were not yet able to receive it. Indeed, even now you are not yet able, for you are still fleshly." Not being able to receive God's truth because of living according to the flesh gives rise to serious sin issues, which the church at Corinth certainly was experiencing. People in the church were even living in incest. Today we see people become dependent upon their pastors or elders for truth and counsel. They can't overcome difficulty, speak out for God's faithfulness, or dispute with an unbeliever for truth because they do not know their Bibles. We have trained people in relational skills and evangelistic strategies, but they don't know the message! They know about believing in Jesus and trusting in Him, but on many other items they fall short. Their lives are riveted with spiritual defeats. They were told that God was supposed to give them a wonderful life, so they have no capacity for processing through a heartbreak or crisis situation. God and His sovereignty over evil is an unknown to them.

We need a well-rounded Christian worldview, which cannot be had without an understanding of the full counsel of God. We need to understand how our faith impacts all of the areas of our lives, culture, and society. Most of all, we need to know our God. Without adequate knowledge, many in the professing church will be deceived. Scripture is given so that we will be "adequate, thoroughly equipped for every good work" (2 Timothy 3:16-17). This takes knowledge, training, an investment of time and energy, and a persistent study of the Word of God. But if we skip the training and teaching, we will be unequipped to do good. The western church could be described as an army going to battle without being armed or armored. Many don't even know that they are in a battle. Revival will be impossible without a transmission of knowledge through the working of the Holy Spirit. Core doctrines unify and sustain the purity of the church over time. They are also essential for refining and reviving the church. We must become acquainted with our God, with His truth, and with His ways. Why would we want to remain infants in Christ when God has a feast of knowing Him prepared for us? Yet many are still babies in Christ, living and walking according to the flesh.

Hosea 4:1 begins with this indictment from God: "Listen to the word of the LORD, O sons of Israel, For the LORD has a case against the inhabitants of the land, Because there is no faithfulness or kindness Or knowledge of God in the land." It says that the Jewish people have so decayed in their understanding and worship of God that they don't even know Him or how to worship Him anymore. In verse 6, God continues, "My people are destroyed for lack of knowledge. Because you have rejected knowledge, I also will reject you from being My priest. Since you have forgotten the law of your God, I also will forget your children." This is serious business. These people chose to reject knowledge, and God rejected them. Their lack of knowledge is what led to their destruction. Even their religious teachers and leaders had rejected knowledge. We can reject knowledge in a couple of ways. For one, we can choose to remain ignorant and not study the Word, being content to be fed the milk of the Word for our entire adult lives. The second way we can reject knowledge is to exchange true spiritual knowledge for the impostor of worldly wisdom, which is foolishness before God. We will think of ourselves as having become wise when in reality we will have become fools. We need to learn from the Word. We are sanctified in the Word, for the word is truth (John 17:17).

John 8:31-32 says, "So Jesus was saying to those Jews who had believed Him, 'If you continue in My word, then you are truly disciples of Mine; and you will know the truth, and the truth will make you free.'" Why are so many people in the church falling into sin or struggling to get out of Satanic temptations and traps? Perhaps it is because they do not have the resources to stand on their own two feet once they leave the Sunday service. We have got to lead people to God's freedom by giving them the truth. We want to be making disciples as the Great Commission has said: "Go therefore and make disciples of all the nations, baptizing them in the name of the Father and the Son and the Holy Spirit, teaching them to observe all that I commanded you; and lo, I am with you always, even to the end of the age" (Matthew 28:19-20). Jesus did not tell us to do whatever we can to get people to profess Christ and make a minimal commitment. Rather, He commanded us to do all that we can by Christ's power to make disciples of men by teaching them the full counsel of God. Christ said to teach them all which He has commanded them. That is a lot to pass on. Sermonettes and preaching aimed only at the "seeker" will not get this done. Churches must be storehouses of knowledge and effective teachers of it. It is no wonder so many Christians doubt their own salvation, living their lives with uncertainty and instability. If we know the teaching of Christ and abide by it, we can know that we are His disciples (1 John 5:13). It is absolutely essential that we view the Bible as God's very words to us, without which we cannot learn, grow, and become mature like Christ.

A Balanced View of Knowledge

Ecclesiastes 12:12 says, "But beyond this, my son, be warned: the writing of many books is endless, and excessive devotion to books is wearying to the body." This is a tip for us from the wisest person ever to live. He says to be warned about writing, reading, and studying too much. He does not condemn any of those activities in and of themselves. He says to just not get too overzealous about building up our knowledge base. The reality is that we have only seventy or so years to live, and there is no point taking in knowledge for that entire period. There needs to be a taking in and a giving out. We must let others benefit from our spiritual knowledge rather than trying to gain knowledge for knowledge's sake. Solomon's advice is that we live a balanced life. 1 Corinthians 8:1-2 says, "Knowledge makes arrogant, but love edifies. If anyone supposes that he knows anything, he has not yet known as he ought to know." In other words, we are to put the emphasis on love and realize the limits of knowledge. In fact, if we think we are so smart and have all the knowledge, we had better wake up and realize that we have missed a foundational point. God has all knowledge, and our knowledge is microscopic compared to His. If we overestimate our knowledge, we need humility because our knowledge has made us arrogant. Knowledge puffs up, so let us keep a balanced perspective of it. We could educate the entire world on the Bible, and they could still miss the simple gospel. We could have all knowledge, but if we have not love, we are nothing (1 Corinthians 13:2). Knowledge alone is not the answer. But a lack of knowledge can be our undoing.

Romans 11:33-36 gives the proper view of knowledge, saying,

"Oh, the depth of the riches both of the wisdom and knowledge of God! How unsearchable are His judgments and unfathomable His ways! For WHO HAS KNOWN THE MIND OF THE LORD, OR WHO BECAME HIS COUNSELOR? Or WHO HAS FIRST GIVEN TO HIM THAT IT MIGHT BE PAID

BACK TO HIM AGAIN? For from Him and through Him and to Him are all things. To Him be the glory forever. Amen."

We must come to a place where we realize that we cannot fully understand God. Deuteronomy 29:29 says, "The secret things belong to the LORD our God, but the things revealed belong to us and to our sons forever, that we may observe all the words of this law." Notice that there are some things that we cannot understand because God has kept them secret. We don't need to know them, for who of us could understand God entirely anyway? What has been revealed to us in the Scripture is for our learning so that we would obey and know what God wants from us in this life. God has not shortchanged us in any way, for we have all that we need for life and godliness. We just need to realize that the lust for knowledge upon knowledge, reading book after book after book, is not the answer. The answer is found in growing in knowledge according to God's Word and communicating that knowledge to others in love.

There are things that we must know. 2 Timothy 2:15 says, "Be diligent to present yourself approved to God as a workman who does not need to be ashamed, accurately handling the word of truth." This ought to be the ambition of all Christians, not just those who are ministers of the gospel. God wants us all to be able to accurately handle God's Word. He wants us to know what to say when a tragedy strikes a family near to us. He wants us to be able to defend the gospel against heresy. He wants us to worship Him in spirit and truth because we know Who it is that we are worshipping.

What If People Won't Listen to Knowledge?

2 Timothy 4:2-5 gives us explicit directions for how we are to handle the time which has come upon us where people do not want to endure sound doctrine and deep-rooted teaching. It says,

> "Preach the word; be ready in season and out of season; reprove, rebuke, exhort, with great patience and instruction. For the time will come when they will not endure sound doctrine; but wanting to have their ears tickled, they will accumulate for themselves teachers in accordance to their own desires, and will

turn away their ears from the truth and will turn aside to myths. But you, be sober in all things, endure hardship, do the work of an evangelist, fulfill your ministry."

When people turn their ears from the full counsel of God and elevate the "knowledge" of man, we must continue to preach the truth and strive to understand God's Word. If this means that church attendance will fall because the Word is preached with authority and in totality, so be it. We must fight for truth and for every Word in the Scriptures. Pastors must be willing to rebuke and exhort their congregations to change or improve in an area. If those who are teachers and preachers of the Word do not give their listeners the truth of God's Word, they will not have fulfilled their ministry. That is serious business before Almighty God.

Information Alone Is Not Enough

Reproving, exhorting, and rebuking involve calling people to action and to response. Educating the world will not save it. Neither will educating Christians as to merely the maps of Paul's missionary journeys and the dates of early church meetings bring them to a place of spiritual maturity. Christians must be shown how God's Word speaks to daily life. Preaching is not a classroom or a mere giving out of information and data, but it is a call to action as God commands in His Word. Good teachers and preachers affect the lives of their learners. They equip their learners to be adequate for whatever good work God calls them to do. Knowledge, data, and information are a part, but there is more to learning than raw information. Wisdom takes knowledge and applies it to life. This is what a good church leader will help his people to do in word and in deed.

All of Scripture Is Essential

The age of postmodernism, moral relativism, and pluralism has rubbed off on the church. It is often said that we should major on the majors and minor on the minors in matters pertaining to Christian doctrine and theology. Other pastors might say that, since it is inevitable that good people will come to different conclusions, we might as well just tolerate a plurality of viewpoints, even if they are directly opposed to one another. This leads churches to tolerate teachings such as theistic evolution or even evolution in the fullest sense of the word since such things are viewed as "minor," "non-essential," or "peripheral" to the "core" doctrines of the faith. Granted, there are certain things that must be believed about the gospel in order for salvation to occur, but the danger becomes when man stands in judgment over God's Word and starts deciding which portions of God's Word he is going to accept. Scripture must stand in judgment over man, not the other way around. The temptation has always been for the church to want to bow to the societal and political pressures of the day to take a view that is popular for the sake of being liked by the world or to win the greater number of followers and listeners. If we stop worrying about what people might think, it is a lot easier to take God's Word at face value and to believe what it says from cover to cover. We cannot afford to read things into the Bible that are not there or to work a "scientific" theory into the text of the Bible. We must let Scripture speak for itself, and science, if it is accurate, will never contradict the Bible.

Some professing Christians go so far as to conclude that it really isn't even worth discussing, analyzing, or working though the "minor" issues such as roles in marriage or theology of the end times because they are just that, "minor." They say that as long as we all believe in Jesus, do the other things really matter? Herein lies the danger of parceling the Scripture into essential and nonessential categories. If everything besides Jesus and the gospel is nonessential, then what motivates us to study the Scriptures to show ourselves approved unto God, workmen that need not be ashamed, rightly dividing the word of truth (2 Timothy 2:15)? If the vast majority of Scripture is really "up for grabs" and not absolutely important, then why did God bother to include it in the first place? Why would He make claims about cursing anyone who adds or subtracts even one word of it (Revelation 22:18-19)? Why would He say that He has inspired all of the Scripture (2 Timothy 3:16)? Why would Paul say that the things written in the Old Testament were for our learning (Romans 15:4)? We must understand that we have no right or authority to categorize the Scripture and to decide what is necessary and what is not. Sure, some things are necessary for salvation while some are not. But how dare we tell God that some part of His revelation to us is irrelevant and extraneous! How dare we pick and choose verses based upon their convenience to us! The danger of placing ourselves as those in authority and judgment over the Scripture is that we then tell God what part of His Word we will accept and what part we will ignore or reject. This denies God's authority and perfection, and it opens the door to a wide variety of fallacies, deceptions, and worldly philosophies.

The point of salvation is not to continue as we are as infants in Christ forever. We are to grow up into Christian adults, attaining to maturity in Christ (Ephesians 4:13-14) and a full assurance of our faith (Hebrews 10:22). If all we ever know are merely the "essentials," God is still merciful to let us into heaven if we put our faith in the right truths. Yet God's intention was never to simply leave us as immature babies who declare that the rest of Scripture is unknowable, irrelevant, boring, or doomed to a plurality of viewpoints no matter what. The reality is that Scripture does have an intended interpretation. Do we honestly think that God wasn't sure what He was trying to say? He put into Scripture exactly what was supposed to be there, every word, phrase, sentence, paragraph, and grammatical subtlety. They are all there for a reason and for our learning. Thus, the entirety of Scripture is necessary and essential and ought to be believed, studied, understood, analyzed, discussed, and contended for. We need to have an appreciation for the whole counsel of God, and together we ought to humbly strive to attain to the unity of the faith, which is only possible as we take the Scripture to mean what God intended it to mean, a difficult and lifelong challenge and task. But it is well worth it, for the only other option is to minimize the importance of Scripture and to tolerate Biblical ignorance and erroneous viewpoints, mistakenly calling such worldly tolerance Christian love. In order to have charity in all things, we must not let go of truth in order to achieve the unity we all desire. Unity of doctrinal truth and Christian love must go hand in hand.

At the end of Hebrews 5, the writer rebuked his readership for needing to receive the milk of the word again rather than being able to move on to more advanced truths and knowledge, which he referred to as eating solid food. He says, beginning in verse 10 and continuing to verse 14,

> "Concerning him [an Old Testament priest named Melchizedek who was a foreshadowing of Christ] we have much to say, and

it is hard to explain, since you have become dull of hearing. For though by this time you ought to be teachers, you have need again for someone to teach you the elementary principles of the oracles of God, and you have come to need milk and not solid food. For everyone who partakes only of milk is not accustomed to the word of righteousness, for he is an infant. But solid food is for the mature, who because of practice have their senses trained to discern good and evil."

The author wanted to give these readers some real solid food to establish them in their faith. They had been saved long enough that they, rather than being dependent upon others for truth, should be able to be teachers of others. Yet they had remained infants in Christ such that they lacked discernment, being even more vulnerable than they were before coming to Christ in that now they think that they are knowledgeable when they really are not. Thus, they are even harder to teach and easier to deceive. The writer refers to the elementary principles of the Word of God as milk fit for infants. In other words, what the modern church has limited to what is essential for us to learn is the same as what relegated these early believers to perpetual infancy, being only able to drink milk. We need to understand that truths about Christ and the gospel are only the introductory elementary principles about Christ and the Christian life. We have to move beyond that.

Hebrews 6:1-3 says,

"Therefore leaving the elementary teaching about the Christ, let us press on to maturity, not laying again a foundation of repentance from dead works and of faith toward God, of instruction about washings and laying on of hands, and the resurrection of the dead and eternal judgment. And this we will do, if God permits."

Interestingly, the writer of Hebrews considered issues such as whether or not ritual cleansings needed to be done now that the New Covenant had been established and things pertaining to the end times to be elementary. These are the things that the modern church considers advanced in nature and not necessary to everyday church life, health, and function because they are difficult and too divisive. Yet the author of Hebrews wanted to move beyond these things to more advanced things. How far we have fallen! The church cannot and will not experience revival until it is willing to humbly labor through the Bible from cover to cover. This is a lifelong calling, but it is one that too many carelessly and callously overlook. Scripture is not always easy to understand, and it takes a lot of work. But unless we study it, we have no chance to seek God's face according to knowledge. This keeps revival at bay. Revival requires that we first believe God's Word is relevant to us in its entirety and that we then begin to obey and apply it. If we don't even believe God's Word, how can we ever expect God to move? When the church begins feasting upon the meat of God's Word, revival will have taken root.

Section 4:

If My People Will "Turn From Their Wicked Ways..."

Section 4

Chapter 8:
What Is True Repentance?

"I have listened and heard, They have spoken what is not right; No man repented of his wickedness, Saying, 'What have I done?' Everyone turned to his course, Like a horse charging into the battle."
Jeremiah 8:6

    To humble oneself is a great challenge considering our desire to be self-made and self-deserving. To pray is an act of boldness and courage for it requires us to believe that it all depends upon God. To seek God's face is a step in the right direction as we seek truth to apply. But to repent is the culminating issue. All has been for naught if we do not let the Spirit of God change us. For revival to occur, repentance must happen. Without repentance there is no salvation or sanctification. Repentance is the stepping stone of growth. God will show us where we come up short, but then we must by faith choose to change and accept His grace at work. We must decide, "Do I follow myself, or do I now follow God as He is leading me?" At this point, we know what step we ought to take. To not take it is sin, and to take it is a step of personal revival. We must decide if we will repent or not, for this is the crisis point for faith.
    2 Chronicles 7:14 describes repentance in a very insightful way. It doesn't even use the word "repentance." It says that we must turn from our wicked ways. Repentance requires that we disown, destroy, and get rid of whatever was sinful. It also requires that we turn toward God. It is a U-turn on the spiritual road of life. It is not good enough to just stop the car from continuing on in the wrong direction, for the car must be spun around and begin heading toward God's direction. If we had usurped the driver's seat, which we did if we were in sin, we must let God take His rightful place of control. Repentance is a complete 180 degree turn.
    The sad part about repentance is that is doesn't get talked about much these days. We talk of asking for forgiveness and accepting Christ, but rarely is repentance used as a part of the gospel message. This is downright wrong and dangerous. Mark 1:14-15 records what

Jesus preached as He began His ministry, saying, "Now after John had been taken into custody, Jesus came into Galilee, preaching the gospel of God, and saying, 'The time is fulfilled, and the kingdom of God is at hand; repent and believe in the gospel.'" It says that Jesus preached the gospel which was to repent and believe that Christ was the Messiah Who had come to save the world. We have no problem with the believing part. We struggle when it comes to repentance. It is an "ouch" word, a word that we are afraid will turn people off or scare them away. But it was Christ's word, and it is a necessary component of saving faith. Can there be saving faith apart from a genuine repentance? Luke 13:5 says, "I tell you, no, but unless you repent, you will all likewise perish." The message is clear. Unless there is repentance of sin and a turning from wicked ways, salvation cannot and will not occur, let alone revival.

Peter, when preaching at Pentecost at the advent of the Holy Spirit, says in Acts 2:37-38,

> "Now when they heard this, they were pierced to the heart, and said to Peter and the rest of the apostles, 'Brethren, what shall we do?' Peter said to them, 'Repent, and each of you be baptized in the name of Jesus Christ for the forgiveness of your sins; and you will receive the gift of the Holy Spirit.'"

These people had heard the gospel message, and they wanted to respond. Should they raise their hand? Should they come forward to the front of the church? Should they kneel in their place? One thing was for sure. They needed to repent. Upon repenting they would be baptized immediately as a public declaration of their faith in Christ and of the washing away of their sins through His blood. They didn't want to wait to show their allegiance. They wanted God's blessing of their obedience and to be welcomed into fellowship with the other believers. Their repentance was what opened their heart to receive the Holy Spirit. The key for the three thousand to be saved was that they repented and turned from their wicked ways and false beliefs to the one true God by faith. Interestingly, the first thing they did was an act of obedience in being baptized. The obedience was a sign of true repentance.

Jesus says in Matthew 3:8, "Therefore bear fruit in keeping with repentance." Repentance has continued outward signs of its reality. It has fruit because obedience follows a turning from sin. Those who have truly repented will have clear signs to show for it.

Godly Sorrow Leads to Repentance

2 Corinthians 7:8-11 says,

> "For though I caused you sorrow by my letter, I do not regret it; though I did regret it--for I see that that letter caused you sorrow, though only for a while-- I now rejoice, not that you were made sorrowful, but that you were made sorrowful to the point of repentance; for you were made sorrowful according to the will of God, so that you might not suffer loss in anything through us. For the sorrow that is according to the will of God produces a repentance without regret, leading to salvation, but the sorrow of the world produces death. For behold what earnestness this very thing, this godly sorrow, has produced in you: what vindication of yourselves, what indignation, what fear, what longing, what zeal, what avenging of wrong! In everything you demonstrated yourselves to be innocent in the matter."

This passage clearly teaches that godly sorrow leads to repentance. Paul had rebuked the Corinthians for various sin issues in his earlier letter. He knew that they had been sorrowful over what they read. This is a good thing, he said, because it was a sign of genuine repentance. They did not regret what they did because they got caught. Rather, they regretted what they did because of genuine repentance. **What is one way to know if a person has experienced genuine repentance? They must ask themselves if they regret what they have done, not merely what happened to them because of it.**

The exciting thing about true repentance is that it produces in us anger at the sin that we fell into, so it motivates us not to go back that way anymore. It also motivates us to encourage others to avoid the same pitfall. It produces in us a healthy fear of God and a fear of the consequences of sin. It also makes us passionate to do right because we see perhaps more obviously and zealously that God's ways are the best ways. To not do God's ways becomes obvious hurt, while to do God's ways becomes obvious joy. Life becomes more black and white, and serving God becomes more of a delight. Such passion and zeal to do what is right is also a sign of a changed heart.

God's Kindness Leads to Repentance

We must understand that the sorrow that the Holy Spirit produces in our hearts when we sin is motivated by God's kindness because He knows what is best for us. Romans 2:4 says, "Or do you think lightly of the riches of His kindness and tolerance and patience, not knowing that the kindness of God leads you to repentance?" The Biblical teaching is that it is when God manifests kindness, grace, and love to us that we are moved to change. There is nothing like a free gift to reveal pride and self-sufficiency, the archenemies of sanctification. Pride wants to earn God's blessings, while God wants to give them freely. What did God do to move us to a restored relationship with Him? Romans 5:8 says, "But God demonstrates His own love toward us, in that while we were yet sinners, Christ died for us." God made the first move and loved us, demonstrating kindness by giving up His own Son for our salvation. As His children, it is His kindness that leads us to repent and turn from our wicked ways, in sanctification just as in salvation.

If only we could see God's kindness in a new and wonderful light and see how much of a joy it is to follow Him with all of our hearts. If only we could see how much of an honor it is to suffer for Him, and if only we could trust Him to help us more frequently live in victory over sin. If only we could see how much He loves us. Ephesians 3:17-19 says,

> "So that Christ may dwell in your hearts through faith; and that you, being rooted and grounded in love, may be able to comprehend with all the saints what is the breadth and length and height and depth, and to know the love of Christ which surpasses knowledge, that you may be filled up to all the fullness of God."

God wants us to spiritually comprehend by faith that His love is boundless and unfathomably great. We can't intellectually process how great God's love and kindness is toward us. It must be received by faith, extrapolating from the love shown by the giving up of His one and only Son. If only we as God's people could see His great love, it would anchor our faith, strengthen our resolve, and move us to increased holiness. When we see and appreciate God's kindness toward us, we will be moved to repent.

Chapter 9:
Return to a Lifestyle of Personal Holiness

"Consecrate yourselves therefore, and be holy, for I am holy."
Leviticus 11:44

What really pleases God in the Christian life? Is it how many verses we have memorized? Is it our Sunday School attendance record? Is it how much money we have given to God? Is it how many people we have influenced to salvation? Is it how many church functions we attend during the week? Is it how many leadership positions we have held? What truly honors God? According to Romans 12:1-2, our spiritual service of worship to God is to present our bodies as living and holy sacrifices to Him. God wants to see hearts that are wholly devoted to Him. He wants to see lives lived for Him on the outside because of an inward heart reality. He wants us to live in obedience to His revealed will. He wants us not to give our bodies, which belong to God and are the dwelling place of the Holy Spirit, to the corruption and filth of the things of the world. Holiness is not about keeping rules and impressing God or others. It is about a sanctification of the heart. Who do we really love? What motivates us? It is all about doing God's will.

Revival cannot and will not happen without Christians committed to holiness. Hebrews 12:14 says, "Pursue peace with all men, and the sanctification without which no one will see the Lord." That we live a holy and sanctified life means everything if we want to impact the lives of others. The world discerns hypocrites faster than we do. They are looking for them constantly because God has set up such a design. They have a reason to deny Christ if His followers do not act like their Master. We cannot afford to blind people from God by our mixed up lifestyles. Titus 2:6-8 says,

> "Likewise urge the young men to be sensible; in all things show yourself to be an example of good deeds, with purity in doctrine, dignified, sound in speech which is beyond reproach, so that the

opponent will be put to shame, having nothing bad to say about us."

Can you imagine a person or a church that gives the world absolutely nothing bad to say about him or them? This puts those who oppose our cause to shame as they are forced to realize that they are the ones with the problem. Our holiness paves the way for gospel truth. How a church tolerates anything less than seriousness about sin is baffling. Too many pastors are content to talk to people about what the people, regenerate or unregenerate, think they need to hear. We have got to get to the heart of the matter. The reality is we have sin problems that need to be dealt with. We usually don't want to hear this, and the ministry of the Word is necessary because sometimes we are unaware of certain sin issues in our lives. Sin must be addressed, in preaching and in evangelism.

Answered prayer is also at stake. Psalm 66:18 says, "If I regard wickedness in my heart, The Lord will not hear." This is a condition of heart when we know we are in the wrong before God, and yet we proudly disregard confessing our sin. We thrust filth into the Holy presence of God. We lose out on intimacy with God because He doesn't answer prayer from a heart in such a condition. This is why personal holiness is so important for a powerful prayer life. Corporate holiness, then, is a factor in a church wide prayer gathering. God wants to see purity in His people. It must be highly insulting to God when we strut into His presence without dealing with our sin in brokenness and contrition. God cannot answer a prayer for revival from an arrogant, divided heart.

God's desire for us is that we bear much fruit (John 15:8). Sin makes such a proficient level of fruit-bearing impossible. God prunes us through loving discipline to help us become more holy in practical living. But it is only those who abide in Christ, which John 15:10 describes as keeping Christ's commandments, who will bear abundant fruit. Do we wonder why we have never seen anybody come to Christ as a result of our testimony? Do we wonder why God is not using us? Do we care that we are not bearing fruit of good deeds and of an inner man filled with the fruit of the Spirit? Do we find that our deeds and characteristics are not building up the kingdom of God? It may be that there is a heart problem of holiness.

We also can't experience the filling of the Holy Spirit if there is sin in the way. A spiritual kingdom must be advanced by spiritual strength and power. We will have none of this if there is sin in our lives. We can forget about being filled with the Spirit if we have forgotten the ways of God. This is a big deal. It is life lived without progress, a full day's work with nothing to show for it, a spinning of the wheels, and vanity. We need the power of the Spirit. Without His filling, we cannot accomplish anything. As John 15:4 says, "Abide in Me, and I in you. As the branch cannot bear fruit of itself unless it abides in the vine, so neither can you unless you abide in Me." We must be one with Christ if we want to see our lives amount to anything of eternal value. We must abide in Him, keeping His ways and maintaining a life of personal holiness.

Matthew 5:23-24 says,

> "Therefore if you are presenting your offering at the altar, and there remember that your brother has something against you, leave your offering there before the altar and go; first be reconciled to your brother, and then come and present your offering."

We are to seek reconciliation and forgiveness with anyone with whom we have unresolved conflict before presenting a sacrifice to God. We don't sacrifice animals on an altar anymore, but we do remember when Christ was sacrificed on the altar of the cross. Before we take communion, which for some churches is every week, we must first deal with any outstanding sin. 1 Corinthians 7:28-30 says,

> "But a man must examine himself, and in so doing he is to eat of the bread and drink of the cup. For he who eats and drinks, eats and drinks judgment to himself if he does not judge the body rightly. For this reason many among you are weak and sick, and a number sleep."

God takes sin seriously. To not deal with sin and yet still participate in the remembrance of Christ's sacrifice is like strutting into God's presence and ignoring the filth of our garments. But in this case God does more than just not listen. He loves His Son and to take His death lightly is worthy of severe discipline. God inflicts His people with illness, weakness, and death because of a misuse of the Lord's Supper. How often do we go to church and make it so casual? We sing "Come, just as you are to worship" and are not mindful of the holiness of God. We think we can be casual and "free" about what we do because we are under grace. Sin does not cut off relationship with God, but it does break intimate fellowship. And it incurs discipline. We cannot dare to be so bold as to blaze into church with filthy garments and think that God doesn't mind that we have come just as we are with a laundry list of sins. It doesn't work that way. Sin must be dealt with. A sinning brother must be confronted. Church discipline must be carried out. We must separate from those who persistently live in rebellion who call themselves Christians (Matthew 18:15-17).

Why is it that we don't care about sin? Perhaps we view God's grace as something to be mocked and abused. Maybe we view sin as a mere mistake or manifestation of human infallibility rather than an abomination before God. Maybe we fail to remember the holiness of God. He will deal with this flagrant neglect of His command to come together with clean hands and pure hearts. Psalm 24:3-4 says, "Who may ascend into the hill of the LORD? And who may stand in His holy place? He who has clean hands and a pure heart." Christ lives in us, and we are the church. As we draw near to His presence corporately on a Sunday morning, it is a great insult to God to draw near to His holy presence with unconfessed sin.

A Compromised Lifestyle

The church really does live in compromise far too often. Hypocrisy can be seen in a variety of ways. Do parents ever quibble and argue before gathering as the church on Sunday morning as they try to get all the kids dressed and out the door? Are things said that need to be dealt with before coming to God in a spirit of worship? How is Saturday night spent? Are the teenagers up late hanging out with their friends doing who knows what? Are they coming prepared for worship or are they totally unfocused, nodding off to sleep during the message?

Why do many Christian parents allow and even encourage their children to operate like the world? James 4:4 says, "You adulteresses, do you not know that friendship with the world is hostility toward God?

Therefore whoever wishes to be a friend of the world makes himself an enemy of God." It is too often the case that there is not much of a difference between "Christian" kids and those who are not saved. The commitment to Christ that is possible for elementary children, middle school students, high school students, and college students just isn't what it could or should be. We are like a sports team making unforced errors, turning the ball over, and shooting ourselves in the foot. The lack of seriousness over sin is extremely disheartening. It is difficult often times to discern between a believer and an unbeliever based upon words and actions. It is usually the T-shirt or bumper sticker about God that is the only thing that sets professing Christians apart.

We need to purge our families of worldly intoxication. Granted, we are in the world and not of it. We are going to be challenged and tempted on every side and from every angle. There is no point in hiding out from it. We need to avoid its influence and be an influence for Christ. Unfortunately, in most cases the culture is winning the influence war. Largely, that is because we succumb to it and because we do not stand for truth.

Consider the principle that God is trying to convey in Exodus 29:10-30. The passage describes the process of consecrating the priests. Aaron and his sons were required to put blood all over the altar and all over their priestly garments. They also had to put some on their right ear lobes, their right thumbs, and on the big toe on their right feet. Looking back from a New Testament perspective where the church is described as a holy priesthood, this has some serious symbolic meaning. The blood of Christ must be applied to what goes in our heads, to what we do and touch, and to where we go. Our entire being must be consecrated to God as a pure and holy sacrifice. We must think only upon what is good, noble, praiseworthy, right, and true. If something is evil and corrupt, we dare not think on it, touch it, do it, or go there. There must be a purging of what is evil, and a consecrating of ourselves for effective priestly service. God had little tolerance for priests who did not follow His expectations exactly, and especially for those who were worldly and corrupt. There is no time for excuses like "boys will be boys," "experience is a great teacher," "we don't want them to be ridiculed by kids at school," "at least he's not like so-and-so's kid," or "everybody else is doing it." Sin is sin, and it needs to be dealt with that way. If children are left to dictate to their parents what they will do, they will treat God the same way. They will have no concept of fearing God. He will be all love and grace. But God is not just all love and grace, and so a lifestyle that exploits grace will have to deal with the consequences of doing so later in life. We must teach our children to follow God early on.

Allurement and Attraction of Material Things

Genesis 4:7 says, "If you do well, will not your countenance be lifted up? And if you do not do well, sin is crouching at the door; and its desire is for you, but you must master it." Satan is a prowling lion seeking whom he may devour (1 Peter 5:8). Maybe he won't lure us into immorality, but perhaps he can master us by distracting us with things. He wants us to view the world in terms of only what our eyes can see. There is more to a given day than just going to work, eating three meals, and putting some money away. There is a spiritual battle going on for souls and for holiness. Sin is crouching at the door. All the devil has to do is distract us from eternal values by letting our eyes only focus on the temporal things, and then sin has mastered us. We can't serve God and wealth (Matthew 6:24). So if we are allured by the here and now, we are not allured by God. It is one way or the other. We need to evaluate our hearts to see if there might be a spiritual bondage to the material things of life.

Christ gives us a remarkably helpful grid by which we can evaluate our lives in terms of our devotion to Him as compared to our attachment to material things. Luke 12:16-21 says,

> "And He told them a parable, saying, 'The land of a rich man was very productive. And he began reasoning to himself, saying, "What shall I do, since I have no place to store my crops?" Then he said, "This is what I will do: I will tear down my barns and build larger ones, and there I will store all my grain and my goods. And I will say to my soul, 'Soul, you have many goods laid up for many years to come; take your ease, eat, drink and be merry.'" But God said to him, "You fool! This very night your soul is required of you; and now who will own what you have

prepared?" So is the man who stores up treasure for himself, and is not rich toward God.'"

For some Christians in America, our job or land has been very productive. We have much more than we need. The temptation is to hoard as much stuff as we can so that we can live off it later and enjoy the good life. There is no Biblical command against saving money for retirement, but there is never a Biblical allowance for retiring from God's work. Many people never retire from God's work because they never began it. We must ask ourselves if we are rich toward God. Have we given much to His church and to ministry in terms of time, energy, and whatever other resources God has given to us? If not, repentance is in order.

Society's Pressure to Activity and Busyness

Jeremiah 29:13 says, "You will seek Me and find Me when you search for Me with all your heart." Many Christians have no idea what this means. Too many are overloading themselves and their children with enormous amounts of activities and busyness. We go from one thing to another to another and to another. There is no time for quiet and meditation before God. There is no time for drawing from His unending resources of strength because we are too busy to do that. We keep going on our own stamina until we fall into pieces. Many people mask this internal fracture for years, while others break down sooner. Those who mask it for long periods of time often break down more severely later on. Life is stressful, and we desperately need God to renew our inner person day by day (2 Corinthians 4:16).

Before Israel had kings and God was King, He gave Israel all kinds of holy days. They would get a day off here and a week off there. Even when Israel had a king, they would dedicate the temple and take a couple weeks off. Later in Nehemiah's time, the people formed a solemn assembly and prayed and worshiped God, repenting of their sin. These people were not worried about their retirement. They were in economic hardship, on the verge of starvation. Yet they had time to stop what they were doing and worship God, taking inventory of their sinful condition before God as they were convicted by His Word. It is hard to imagine a church taking a day, let alone a week, to be before God as an assembly together seeking His will, reading His Word, and praising His name. The fact of the matter is that we need time off to meditate on God and to reflect upon what He is doing in our lives and upon what He wants to do. We need rest. God took rest on the Sabbath. The Sabbath principle is that we need to take regular, weekly rest as well.

Do we want to hear from God? Do we want to be revived? Let's take the cell phone away from our ears for ten minutes. Let's turn the radio off for once as we drive. We can skip a night with our friends and find a quiet spot to meditate on God's Word. We are citizens of another country. We need to give faith an opportunity to bring that reality to mind and to focus on the priorities of the kingdom. **Our busyness keeps revival at bay because it keeps God away.**

Victory Is Ours In Christ

The good news is that we can live in victory over sin (Romans 8:12-13). We are not forced to obey our fleshly desires. The person who walks in the way of the Spirit is putting to death the deeds of the flesh. This is where true life is found, not in seeing how close we can get to the fire without getting burned. Our God is a consuming fire. We ought rather to fear His fiery judgment as it will one day reveal what has been done in the flesh versus what has been done in the Spirit.

Before we were saved, Satan literally had us captive. It would be like having a chain wrapped around our ankles. We were Satan's minions, and we had to do what he wanted and go where he wanted. When we repented and trusted in Christ for salvation, that chain was shattered and broken. Satan has no power over us any longer. Yet we live as if we are chained to the power of sin and death. 1 Corinthians 10:13 says,

> "No temptation has overtaken you but such as is common to man; and God is faithful, who will not allow you to be tempted beyond what you are able, but with the temptation will provide the way of escape also, so that you will be able to endure it."

We are all tempted, and inevitably we will all stumble (James 3:2). The promise of God, however, is that God is faithful to bring us through temptation without our having to give in to sin. Our weakness is that we try to endure and escape by our own power and means when we need to escape through Christ's power. We are to do all things through Christ who strengthens us, including resisting and overcoming temptation. We can walk in victory over sin if we keep faith in Christ's victory over sin strong in our hearts. Though our strength will fail, His victory never will. We must live according to His strength. This is how we can live in victory and be revived.

Too many Christians live as if they are still chained to the devil and enslaved to the power of sin. Many trudge into church on Sunday after another week of defeats. What could happen if they understood how to win that battle? What if they trusted in Christ and not in their own efforts? Families would change, churches would change, and eventually communities, societies, and culture would be impacted.

It all comes down to repentance. If we repent, revival can come. We must humble ourselves, pray, seek God's face, and repent. This is the culmination, the outworking of faith, and the beginning of revival.

Chapter 10:

Cultivate Corporate Holiness

"You also, as living stones, are being built up as a spiritual house for a holy priesthood, to offer up spiritual sacrifices acceptable to God through Jesus Christ."
1 Peter 2:5

God will judge each of His children based upon how we have invested in the kingdom, but very rarely do we think of God evaluating the quality of service and commitment of a local church as a corporate body. If God was writing a letter to the pastor or to an elder of our church, what would it say? Even if our church has the appearance of success or morality, what would God say? God told five of the seven churches in Revelation that they must repent. Only to the church at Smyrna and Philadelphia did God give a complete commendation and an encouraging word of sustenance, provision, protection, and blessing. To Philadelphia He spoke of giving them an open door which no one could shut. That would be a great promise to have from God Himself about the continuation of effective ministry into the future. Unfortunately, five churches didn't have such a healthy prognosis. In fact, God told them to repent or lose their lampstand, a serious threat and indictment from Almighty God.

God can dissolve a church in a second. It can divide, it can be corrupted, it can become apostate and deny the faith, or people can just stop coming. Perhaps there are no converts for years, and so the regular attendees gradually die off. God can destroy a church in many ways, and we don't know exactly how He would remove His lampstand. Perhaps He would just make a church ineffective. How many churches are there along a block in our cities and towns that have never made a dent in the community as an influence for Christ? How many churches do not preach the Word? How many churches have denied the simplicity of devotion to Christ? Many churches exist in this country with no lampstand. Some don't exist any more at all. We must ask ourselves, especially if we are in positions of influence and leadership, if our churches are in jeopardy of having their lampstands removed.

Going Through the Motions at Ephesus

To the church at Ephesus, God says in Revelation 2:1-5,

"To the angel of the church in Ephesus write: The One who holds the seven stars in His right hand, the One who walks among the seven golden lampstands, says this: 'I know your deeds and your toil and perseverance, and that you cannot tolerate evil men, and you put to the test those who call themselves apostles, and they are not, and you found them to be false; and you have perseverance and have endured for My name's sake, and have not grown weary. But I have this against you, that you have left your first love. Therefore remember from where you have fallen, and repent and do the deeds you did at first; or else I am coming to you and will remove your lampstand out of its place--unless you repent."

This is a hard-working church with many laborers. Many in the church were mature Christians who were well-versed in the truth of Christ, even able to discern false teachers. They were so true to their doctrine that they even excommunicated the false teachers. Unlike many churches in our day, they had no tolerance for evil men. They were persistent in their service and ministry, doing all of the right church activities. But God rebuked them and twice told them to repent because they had lost their first love. If God is not the supreme object of our devotion, then our lampstand is in jeopardy unless we repent. We shall have no other gods before Him. God is not into half-hearted worship or diligent service that neglects a love of Him above all else. Just because we go to church every week or sign up for a variety of ministries does not mean that we love God. We really need a reality check here. How easy is it for us to be Ephesus and fall for this! Indeed, it is possible to worship church above Christ. Let us learn from Ephesus before it is too late. God has always been more interested in our hearts than in what we do for Him or in His name.

Devoid of Doctrine and Discipline at Pergamum

To the church at Pergamum, God says in Revelation 2:12-16,

> "And to the angel of the church in Pergamum write: The One who has the sharp two-edged sword says this: I know where you dwell, where Satan's throne is; and you hold fast My name, and did not deny My faith even in the days of Antipas, My witness, My faithful one, who was killed among you, where Satan dwells. But I have a few things against you, because you have there some who hold the teaching of Balaam, who kept teaching Balak to put a stumbling block before the sons of Israel, to eat things sacrificed to idols and to commit acts of immorality. So you also have some who in the same way hold the teaching of the Nicolaitans. Therefore repent; or else I am coming to you quickly, and I will make war against them with the sword of My mouth."

If we think our area is difficult to reach with the gospel, we should try living in Pergamum. It was said by God to be the throne room of Satan. There must have been some really awful things going on there, such as the idolatry and immorality that is referred to. A few in the church had given in to the surrounding culture and to Nicolas, a church father who was not much of one, advocating free love and license in matters of Christian conduct. God commended the church for holding fast to the truth despite the harsh environment. Yet He told the church to repent and deal with the sin in the congregation, or else He would harshly deal with those people Himself.

We need to look at our churches and see if we are permitting false doctrines to be taught by some in the congregation. If there are those who continue in such destructive beliefs, we need to apply church discipline, and if need be, excommunicate them until Satan can deal with them. We need to repent if we are allowing license to sin and abusing the grace of God. If we are not drawing a line in the sand on issues of clear right and wrong and doctrinal purity, we need to repent.

Toleration of Sin in Thyatira

To the church at Thyatira in Revelation 2:18-22, God says,

"And to the angel of the church in Thyatira write: The Son of God, who has eyes like a flame of fire, and His feet are like burnished bronze, says this: 'I know your deeds, and your love and faith and service and perseverance, and that your deeds of late are greater than at first. But I have this against you, that you tolerate the woman Jezebel, who calls herself a prophetess, and she teaches and leads My bond-servants astray so that they commit acts of immorality and eat things sacrificed to idols. I gave her time to repent, and she does not want to repent of her immorality. Behold, I will throw her on a bed of sickness, and those who commit adultery with her into great tribulation, unless they repent of her deeds.'"

To the rest of the church God said in verse 24 that He had no other burden to place on them. They were serving faithfully and improving in their deeds and devotion. He only had one issue, and that is because they tolerated the false teaching of a particular woman in the church. She considered herself a prophetess, but she led the sheep astray like Jezebel of the Old Testament. False teaching always has negative effects, leading to immorality and idolatry, and this case was no exception. God gave this false teacher time to repent, but she had not. Unless she and those who had fallen for her deception repented, they were going to experience great pain. The church itself must repent from their toleration of this woman.

A little leaven leavens the whole lump of dough (Galatians 5:9). This is the principle here. The church at Thyatira passed God's evaluation except for one point: they tolerated a false teacher. This is a very similar problem to the church at Pergamum, which also had false teaching invading the church. Pergamum had it more severely because of several different sects. Here it all came down to one woman. If they would excommunicate her, all would be solved. But they tolerated her, and she led many in the church astray. It is interesting that the same problem is repeated in two of the seven churches. Evidently, false teaching is one of the major things that any church will have to deal with. Both Scripture and experience show that this is indeed the case. This is why the Scripture must be studied carefully through and through and from cover to cover.

In the case of Thyatira, it would appear that the church had a firm doctrinal position, yet they tolerated when one person deviated from their declared beliefs. The danger in this is that sheep are vulnerable animals and are easily led astray. We could all testify as to how we have been deceived in our lives. It is not that hard to pull off a con if a person really wants to do it, especially if Satan is behind it. In an instance of false teaching like this one, this person needed to be confronted by the leadership immediately. If she did not recant, she needed to be removed from the church.

In the church, we cannot tolerate corruption and deception. We must speak the truth in love. Love tells people the reality of their error but not judgmentally or self-righteously. It is tactful and delicate but straightforward and bold. In terms of absolute truth, God is not into diversity like the world is into diversity. He doesn't try to find common ground with false teaching. He doesn't tolerate anything that contradicts His character or will. His way is the only right way, and His truth is the only truth. When a spirit of toleration of false teaching creeps into our churches, we are in danger. God calls such a body to repent and seek fast His Word and His truth.

Spiritually Sleeping At Sardis

To the church at Sardis in Revelation 3:1-4 God says,

> "To the angel of the church in Sardis write: He who has the seven Spirits of God and the seven stars, says this: 'I know your deeds, that you have a name that you are alive, but you are dead. Wake up, and strengthen the things that remain, which were about to die; for I have not found your deeds completed in the sight of My God. So remember what you have received and heard; and keep it, and repent. Therefore if you do not wake up, I will come like a thief, and you will not know at what hour I will come to you. But you have a few people in Sardis who have not

soiled their garments; and they will walk with Me in white, for they are worthy."

These people had a solid foundation of truth, and they appeared to have had an excellent past with a reputation for being vibrant and alive. But God knew that they were largely dead, and the parts that were still alive were about to die. His charge was for them to return to their foundations and repent. Only a few people in the church had not become spiritually dead. God charged them to wake up from their sinful sedation and falling away from foundational truths. This body was in desperate need of revival.

Ephesians 5:14 says, "For this reason it says, 'Awake, sleeper, And arise from the dead, And Christ will shine on you.'" 1 Thessalonians 5:6 says, "So then let us not sleep as others do, but let us be alert and sober." Many churches have Bibles in the pews and a solid doctrinal statement, yet they are dead. Perhaps the gospel is no longer preached, or maybe it has been modified by new leadership. Maybe the pastor is afraid to call out specific sin issues in the church and preach against them. Then again, as in many modern churches, perhaps the church leadership is afraid to stand for truth. A church that bears no fruit is as good as dead. It is without a doubt the case that inside many church walls sit many who are not going to heaven. At Sardis, a few people had not participated in the falling away from truth and the corruption of their lifestyles. But their faithfulness was not enough to stave off the judgment of God. God wanted to hold those responsible who had not been faithful, and He was sure to reward those who had not compromised. We need to make sure that we are those who have not soiled our garments. The church needs a spiritual awakening, returning to a simple belief and commitment to Christ and His teaching. Those who are awake must remain sober so that the deceitfulness of sin doesn't lead them astray as well. We must always be alert for Satan's ploys lest we become corrupted without even realizing what has happened to us. Bold preaching and pure living are central to keeping us on track.

Lukewarm and Lazy at Laodicea

To the church at Laodicea, God says in Revelation 3:14-20,

"To the angel of the church in Laodicea write: The Amen, the faithful and true Witness, the Beginning of the creation of God, says this: 'I know your deeds, that you are neither cold nor hot; I wish that you were cold or hot. So because you are lukewarm, and neither hot nor cold, I will spit you out of My mouth. Because you say, "I am rich, and have become wealthy, and have need of nothing," and you do not know that you are wretched and miserable and poor and blind and naked, I advise you to buy from Me gold refined by fire so that you may become rich, and white garments so that you may clothe yourself, and that the shame of your nakedness will not be revealed; and eye salve to anoint your eyes so that you may see. Those whom I love, I reprove and discipline; therefore be zealous and repent. Behold, I stand at the door and knock; if anyone hears My voice and opens the door, I will come in to him and will dine with him, and he with Me.'"

It seems that the Laodiceans thought that they were all right. In fact, they believed that they were so well off that they didn't think they even needed God. God quoted their own words back to them as an indictment, reminding them that they believed that they had need of nothing, including God. It is easy for a church that is wealthy or prosperous to think that it doesn't need God anymore. It is easy to begin to believe that our methods, formulas, strategies, programs, and seven step plans are sufficient to reach the world with the true gospel. God warned the Laodiceans that they made Him so nauseated that He was going to vomit them out of His mouth. He hates self-sufficiency because He and His Word alone are sufficient for life and ministry. God wants people who are two things according to this passage. First, He wants people who are full of passion, energetic, enthusiastic, willing to place their lives on the line, and committed to the end. God wants zeal. The Laodiceans, on the other hand, were indifferent, perhaps lazy. They thought they were good as they were. They had set up camp and decided to enjoy the good life. Likely they didn't want to be bothered with evangelism because it's messy and with prayer because it is for amateurs who don't know how to operate in God's kingdom. They may have been successful entrepreneurs in society, yet God rebuked them for bringing that mindset into the church. The second thing God indicted them for was being wishy-washy. He wanted people who were totally committed to His will and purposes and to drawing strength and confidence from Him. These people in their self-sufficiency were not useful to God. He told them to buy gold, white clothes, and eye salve from Him, rather than being confident in what their own hands could produce. He shouted to them, "You need me!" Yet they were all right as they were, or so they thought. God hates it when those who profess to know and love Him walk a sort of "middle ground" of spirituality. They have one eye on the kingdom and one eye on their pet sin. Since man cannot serve two masters at one time, the sin ends up winning out. Sin always sickens God, but it is even more distasteful to Him when the person in sin claims to love God at the same time, perhaps even participating in a variety of church functions or positions. God will bring discipline if the church doesn't do its job of correcting the one in sin. Lukewarm Christianity is a cancer, for it leads some to sinful destruction and others to a false hope of salvation. God calls us to be pure before Him and to depend fully upon Him. He wants people full of life, zeal, and energy, ready and eager to do His will. Churches filled with people who are eager to obey are few and far between. Revival is definitely needed.

Final Thought

Joshua 7 records the sad story of Achan. Israel had just conquered the massive walled city of Jericho simply by faith and the blowing of trumpets. Israel continued on confidently up to the much smaller and weaker city of Ai, and they were defeated. They were flabbergasted and confused. Something must have been wrong. Joshua inquired of the Lord, and the Lord told Him that sin was the problem. The people were to consecrate themselves the next morning and gather in tribes and families. God picked a tribe and then a family. Achan was singled out. He admitted his sin, which was disobeying God's command not to keep any of the spoil of the pagan peoples. But God was angry. He had Achan and all of his family stoned and burned, sending a very clear message about the seriousness of sin. If Israel disobeyed Him, they would face severe consequences, even death.

The scary thing about the story is that one man's sin cost his entire family their lives. And not only that, but it cost the entire nation of Israel, which represented millions of people, a battle, compromising their ability to invade the land effectively and efficiently. This is a picture of sin in the New Testament church. One sin in the body can destroy the effectiveness for advancing the kingdom of God. This is hard to get our minds around because we often think of ourselves as individuals who gather together on Sunday morning. But we are a body, and when one goes down, the rest of us are affected. Our testimony is hampered. It makes us question, doubt, re-evaluate, and wonder. This is why God deals so harshly with Achan. If we want to be effective as corporate bodies of believers in our local churches, we really need to be mindful of sin. When one falls, the entire body will be disadvantaged. This is why Hebrews 10:24-25 says, "And let us consider how to stimulate one another to love and good deeds, not forsaking our own assembling together, as is the habit of some, but encouraging one another; and all the more as you see the day drawing near." We need the support. We must help a sinning brother and restore him, not judge him or condemn him. The mission is to stimulate one another to good deeds and holiness. Encouragement is the operative word and not judgment. However, if sin persists, church discipline must follow. Let us not overlook the seriousness of even one person's sin in terms of its affect upon an entire congregation. When God's power and blessing seem to be missing, we must ask ourselves if sin is the problem.

Chapter 11:
Evangelize Biblically

"But you will receive power when the Holy Spirit has come upon you; and you shall be My witnesses both in Jerusalem, and in all Judea and Samaria, and even to the remotest part of the earth."
Acts 1:8

Most Christians never share their faith. Very few have shared with one person in the last year. This is a major problem for the church. Some poor theology has crept in which has led to this problem. For others it is a sin issue, and it needs to be repented of. James 4:17 says, "Therefore, to one who knows the right thing to do and does not do it, to him it is sin." We need to deal with our lack of evangelism as a sin issue before God. We need to repent over our lack of faithfulness to God's command and commission. But there are many reasons that people do not witness, and we want to remove those roadblocks to this important area of Christian maturity.

If we want to see revival, we must take our hearts which have been humbled before God and broken for the lost and begin to share our faith. If our hearts are not broken over the lost to the point where we feel like we have to do something about it, there is a problem somewhere. It all starts with a brokenness over the souls of the lost because of a conviction of their eternal destiny in hell. In a day where proselytizing is getting a bad name, we cannot cease evangelizing.

The Power Is in the Word and through the Spirit

1 Corinthians 1:17, 21 says,

"For Christ did not send me to baptize, but to preach the gospel, not in cleverness of speech, so that the cross of Christ would not be made void. For since in the wisdom of God the world through its wisdom did not come to know God, God was well-pleased through the foolishness of the message preached to save those who believe."

If any man tries to win somebody to Christ by their own cleverness of speech, they are making the cross of Christ devoid of power. Spiritual battles must be fought with spiritual means by spiritual power in Christ. Smooth speaking and a great sale's pitch isn't going to get the job done. That doesn't mean that we shouldn't develop a conversational ability in sharing the gospel, but we cannot rely on it. Nor can it distract from the simple gospel message. The world through its wisdom cannot find God. It is through a foolish message preached that some will be saved.

Many say preaching is obsolete because it is a monologue, and monologues are one of the least effective teaching methodologies. Others will tell you that the art of street evangelism and door to door evangelism is outdated because of culture, or they will tell you that you are a fool for doing it the old-fashioned way. The reality is that, in both evangelism and preaching, there is an interaction of the Holy Spirit with the speaker, the Holy Spirit is working on the listener, and the Word of God is exercising its power as well. It is much more than a monologue or sales presentation. There is a spiritual dynamic present. The world through its wisdom cannot find God. This is why if we appeal to the flesh and to the desires of the natural man to want to come to church because they hear their secular music, because they are entertained with stories, because they are fed a watered down gospel about believe and receive with no repentance, or because they can make church their version of a club, we are doing them a great disservice. In fact, we may be seeing multitudes of false conversions.

God has chosen to vest His power in the gospel, in preaching, in His Word, and in weakness. Society tells us we are fools to believe in any of these. Some in the church are beginning to think so as well. 1 Corinthians 2:4-5 says, "And my message and my preaching were not in persuasive words of wisdom, but in demonstration of the Spirit and of power, so that your faith would not rest on the wisdom of men, but on the power of God." Think how many professions of faith rest upon the wisdom of men and not the power of God. Conferences are held every year training people to use worldly wisdom to generate faith. This was not Paul's way, and with his knowledge base and communication skills,

He certainly could have done so if he had believed it worthwhile. His choice of words, his language, his style, his methodology, his presentation techniques, and his content were not made to entice, sell, or persuade based upon worldly wisdom and worldly-based sales techniques. He did not emotionally manipulate or lure through fleshly mentalities. He did not rely upon the latest facilities, spotlights, and stage sets which pop artists would envy. He made it simple. God was the center, and the gospel message was the point. It was not about Paul or a specific church, but it was all about getting the gospel message out. The result of a "faith" based upon clever techniques is a faith based upon the wisdom of men and not the power of God. This could very likely result in a false conversion. We need to take this principle seriously. People need to encounter the Spirit of God which they will if they are preached the Word of truth. Romans 1:16 says, "For I am not ashamed of the gospel, for it is the power of God for salvation to everyone who believes, to the Jew first and also to the Greek." Is a clever presenter the power of God to salvation? Is coming up with analogies and illustrations that supposedly are required to help a post-modern, post-Christian culture understand the gospel the power of God to salvation? Or is it a simple declaration of the Word of God? We are not talking about passion-less preaching or a lack of preparation. We are talking about the sufficiency of the Word of God to accomplish what it has set out to do. **It is a humbling truth to admit that the Word has the power and that the Spirit's role is more potent than our own clever manipulations. But it is the reality.**

1 Corinthians 4:20 says, "For the kingdom of God does not consist in words but in power." It's not ultimately a debate or discussion that will lead somebody to Christ. It is the Holy Spirit at work behind the scenes opening up a heart and keeping Satan's delusions at bay. We can be certain that there is a spiritual war for each and every soul. We must remember that there is more going on than we can perceive with our physical senses. It is not just that a person is stubborn, but the reality is that he is a captive of the devil. It is not just that he disagrees with the gospel, but he is an ally of Satan. We must be sensitive to and filled with the Holy Spirit as we witness. We must elevate the importance of prayer in evangelism. And if we want to see revival, we must elevate the Word of God and decrease ourselves because the Word carries power. The

message is so simple and so powerful in and of itself that it is a wonder that we have to add to it and pretty it up so much. Perhaps we so want results which impress the Christian community that we will do whatever we can to get them. Pragmatism, believing that results justify methods, is sin, and it must stop being a pattern of operation in the church.

We can't buy off the Spirit to move in a person's heart to convict them. We cannot use our cleverness and beautiful building and stylistic preaching to make the Spirit convict the hearts and souls of men. Too many churches work so hard on the presentation that they minimize the message. Some people are really good in their flesh, and they masquerade it as innovation and creativity. The reality is that we are messengers. The power is not in the messenger but in the message. A letter carrier does not open mail and add to it or take away from what is written. Nor do they edit out the difficult parts and rewrite things to be more palatable for the owner of the envelope. Their job is simply to deliver the message. Opening the letter is illegal for the postal carrier, and it is wrong for the preacher and evangelist to tamper with God's Word as well. We are not to change one word of it unless we want to risk the severe judgment of God. We cannot use Scripture to preach our agenda or adapt Scripture to say what we want it to say. We are simply to deliver the message and the meaning of the text.

We must pray for the working of God to prepare the soil of men's hearts to receive truth as we share the gospel through the Word of God. Without the Spirit moving, we have no chance and no power. If we want to see Him move by convicting hearts of sin, by opening hearts to truth, and by way of providing opportunities for sharing our faith, we must pray. God's Word can cut a person to the core. We must put a priority on communicating Bible verses in evangelism. The power is in God's Word. An illustration can help support the Word, but the Word must be shared.

Sending, Preaching, Hearing, Saving

The Word of God can stand on its own. Romans 10:13-17 says,

"For 'WHOEVER WILL CALL ON THE NAME OF THE LORD WILL BE SAVED.' How then will they call on Him in whom they have not believed? How will they believe in Him whom they have not heard? And how will they hear without a preacher? How will they preach unless they are sent? Just as it is written, 'HOW BEAUTIFUL ARE THE FEET OF THOSE WHO BRING GOOD NEWS OF GOOD THINGS!' However, they did not all heed the good news; for Isaiah says, 'LORD, WHO HAS BELIEVED OUR REPORT?' So faith comes from hearing, and hearing by the word of Christ."

This Scripture passage ought to be a major pillar of any church's evangelistic philosophy. Faith comes by hearing the word of Christ. It is the Word of God and the gospel message that is the cause of the salvation effect. It is not us directly, though we must incarnate the love of Christ. It is ultimately the Word of God that will convict the unsaved of sin and help them to change. We cannot shy away from using Scripture in our evangelism for fear that we might offend someone. If someone is offended, we can shake the dust off our feet and move on. Our duty is simply to declare the truth. Our lives ought to make people interested in the gospel, and they certainly shouldn't contradict any gospel truths. But faith comes by hearing the Word of God. **Our lives carry enormous weight in creating an audience for the gospel, but ultimately we need to share the message. Faith comes by hearing that message.**

Nobody gets saved unless they hear, nobody will hear unless they are preached to, and nobody will preach the gospel unless they are sent. In one sense we are all sent in that we are commissioned by Christ Himself to share the gospel. Yet the local church ought to be sending people out into the community to share the truth of the gospel. It doesn't say to bring them to the preacher, though there is nothing wrong with inviting somebody to observe church. Yet how will we even invite a person to church unless we have gone to them. We must go to them; it is up to us to take the initiative.

The Church Confused and Unequipped

The sad thing today is that there is so much confusion about the message itself. The sadder thing is that so many Christians don't even know the gospel message. Even worse, since they don't know it, they rely on their pastor or a church service to save somebody, and they never share their faith. Our mission field is at least our sphere of influence. This may include our family and extended family, friends, co-workers, neighbors, and anybody else we run into regularly. Store clerks and waitresses could be given a tract, as long as the testimony kept before them is pure. That one tract may be the only chance these people will ever have to hear the truth of the gospel. But if we don't know it, cannot present it, or our lives eliminate us from being legitimate in sharing it, we have kept that person destined for eternity in hell. There is much at stake here. This is a serious issue for the church.

Christian Maturity Includes Reproducing Faith

Many evaluate Christian maturity based upon an increasing knowledge of Christ. They are right to do so, as long as that knowledge is impacting their lives. Others measure spirituality by godliness, which is also a correct component. But there is another element to Christian maturity. When a tree reaches maturity, it bears its fruit in season and sows seeds to reproduce itself. Similarly, if we are growing to maturity, we ought also to be bearing fruit, some of which will be in influencing others toward Christ. As we share the Word of God, we may plant seeds, or we may water seeds planted by others. In either case, it is ultimately God Who gives the growth. But, one way or another, we are to be sowing the seeds of the gospel in the hearts of men.

"Seeker-sensitive" Is Loving

Seeker-sensitive, seeker-targeted, and seeker-friendly are terms thrown around today with significant variance in meaning. For our purposes, seeker-targeted describes a church that constructs a service based upon the needs of the consumer, the seeker. Seeker-friendly would be very much the same, gearing the church environment to be more palatable to the unregenerate mind and soul, a dangerous task and in some ways abominable. Seeker-sensitive is merely an acknowledgement that unsaved people are welcome at church, though not welcome to participate in the Lord's Supper. Without detracting from the reality that church is a community of the saved, churches that are seeker-sensitive in the Biblical sense of the word try to do a good job at welcoming the visitors and being sure that the gospel is clearly presented. The message is preached to believers, though it might be prefaced by encouraging a visitor to grab a Bible from the pew, for example. It is merely being sensitive, hospitable, and loving.

The term "seeker" also needs to be defined. Although no one seeks God of their own initiative (Romans 3:11), the Holy Spirit does draw people (Matthew 22:14). These "drawees" have falsely been labeled seekers, likely because of the increased reliance on man-made methods to influence salvation rather than trusting in the Spirit of God to move as He would. John 3:21 says, "But he who practices the truth comes to the Light, so that his deeds may be manifested as having been wrought in God." God always gets the credit for salvation, but we can encourage people to practice the truth.

It is possible that some who have developed the seeker-targeted mentality did so from pure motives, desiring to see the gospel more clearly presented to the lost. They may have become frustrated with churches that are not sensitive to the seeker. In a typical insensitive church, the pastor speaks in Christianese, talking over the head of the unbeliever who is visiting or invited by a Christian friend. Even if the gospel was presented, it would be explained in a way that is so theologically involved that it will make no sense to the unbeliever. The music might be so outdated and dull that it is distracting from genuine Spirit-led worship. The atmosphere might be old, ugly, dank and dingy, or just plain tacky. The congregation is a "holy huddle," not wanting any newcomers or "unclean" people to come in and wreck their "purity." The visitor goes without a greeting from anyone other than a detached, unloving handshake as they are given a bulletin. Those who proclaim seeker-targeted strategies have revolted and thrown the pendulum too far to the other side.

In a seeker-sensitive church, the gospel is not watered down or minimized, but complex theological ideas are at least defined and explained. There is no merit to wanting to share the gospel without at least trying to explain what we are talking about. As visitors come in, we should be sensitive to them in how we greet them and welcome them. It is an ugly thing when churches pressure visitors to raise their hand, get some literature, or stand up so others can applaud them for coming. These things are just plain embarrassing and foolish. Many Christians are out of practice in relating to strangers, especially to potentially unsaved strangers. We just need to talk to them as those who truly care about them, giving them space while making ourselves available to answer questions that they might have. It should be clear to them that we do not indulge in the sins that they love, but it should also be evident that that does not mean that we look down upon them. As God leads us, we need to have the courage to speak out concerning our Savior. It is not good enough just to be nice, for the message is what saves.

Some seeker-sensitive churches provide visitors with a Bible, which they can either return or keep at the end of the service. Some have a few ushers walk the aisles and give people Bibles as needed. When turning to a passage of Scripture, they tell them where to find it. Passing an offering plate can make those who don't give uncomfortable, and it encourages others to judgmentally watch who gives and who doesn't. A seeker-sensitive church might place a box in the back of the sanctuary into which people can drop their offerings as they come or go. When the Lord's Supper is observed, a seeker-sensitive church is careful to explain who it is for and what it is about. The Lord's Supper is a great opportunity to present the gospel without the service becoming entirely evangelistically focused. The pastor can do a great deal in making people feel welcome and in creating an atmosphere conducive to relaxed conversation about God and truth. The truth may not be relaxing or unthreatening, but the manner in which it is conveyed can be as loving as possible. The pastor himself must be very comfortable being around the unsaved, and he ought to provide a great example of relating to them in love, truth, and grace. We need to be sensitive to the needs of people as they visit with us. Christ would have. He would have associated with them and shared the truth with them, never backing down. He always met people where they were at. If we desire to truly love a person who is seeking the truth, there is no excuse for being insensitive to their needs.

Being Biblically seeker-sensitive can be seen in 1 Corinthians 9:16-24, which says,

> "For if I preach the gospel, I have nothing to boast of, for I am under compulsion; for woe is me if I do not preach the gospel.

For if I do this voluntarily, I have a reward; but if against my will, I have a stewardship entrusted to me. What then is my reward? That, when I preach the gospel, I may offer the gospel without charge, so as not to make full use of my right in the gospel. For though I am free from all men, I have made myself a slave to all, so that I may win more. To the Jews I became as a Jew, so that I might win Jews; to those who are under the Law, as under the Law though not being myself under the Law, so that I might win those who are under the Law; to those who are without law, as without law, though not being without the law of God but under the law of Christ, so that I might win those who are without law. To the weak I became weak, that I might win the weak; I have become all things to all men, so that I may by all means save some. I do all things for the sake of the gospel, so that I may become a fellow partaker of it. Do you not know that those who run in a race all run, but only one receives the prize? Run in such a way that you may win."

Seeker-sensitive is written all over Paul's heart in this passage. His heart and passion for the gospel is deeply moving. Paul was not worried about people approving of him or of his preaching. He preached it like it was. Seeker-sensitive does not cater to the lost; rather, it is just building a bridge to them by connecting God's Word to their world. In no way does being seeker-sensitive involve putting ourselves in compromising situations or tolerating sin. Neither does it ever allow us to compromise the totality of God's Word or to hold back from preaching it with full boldness. For example, preaching to slaves, Paul likely talked about being slaves of righteousness. Preaching to Jews, he probably explained the purpose of the Law. Preaching to Gentiles, he educated himself on their religious beliefs and then showed them how Jesus was the One Whom they had been looking for all along (Acts 17:16-34). He was sensitive to where each of his audiences was coming from.

Paul saw himself as completely worthless, defeated, and undone if he did not share his faith. So should we. If he shared his faith willingly with a good attitude, it would be for eternal rewards, not monetary rewards for the here and now. If he did it because he felt he ought to, but his heart was not in it, he was being a steward of what was entrusted to him. Paul spoke of making himself a slave to all men. That means that he was willing to put the interests of others ahead of his own. It is like a missionary going into a foreign culture and adopting their customs and dress all the while not violating the commands of God. Paul never compromised the Word, and being seeker-sensitive must never compromise the Word. Creating a church atmosphere that is seeker-targeted, which by definition must appeal to carnal appetites and must try to change the message by eradicating the inherent offense of the cross, is not what Paul is advocating here. He became all things to all men for the purpose of winning some. He didn't tell a person to stop the drinking habit and dress in a shirt and tie before coming to church. He wanted them to come as they were, but to leave changed. His message was never to boost their self-esteem, but it was to destroy self-reliance and to challenge them to deny themselves. It is possible to be both loving and bold at the same time. **Being all things to all people does not allow us to create whatever kind of style we want or to separate ourselves from sound doctrine. It is merely going out of our way to be kind to people all within a context of the declaration of truth.**

It is much easier to drop the evangelistic focus of a Sunday morning or to feel self-righteous about preaching the gospel to the choir every week. Yet the congregation is aware of the hypocrisy and an environment of separation is being created. We cannot afford to separate from the culture such that we alienate people and fail to share the gospel. The seeker-sensitive mode is harder, but it is consistent with the early church and with God's Word.

Prepare, Practice, Preach

It is very important that we think through what the gospel message is all about. In fact, if more churches would offer an evangelistic training program for their people, excuses for not sharing the gospel would lessen, and more mouths would be open for the gospel. The alarm must be sounded as loud as possible to wake up pastors, church leaders, and parents to the fact that most people in today's churches are unable and unequipped to be able to share their faith. What does the Scripture say about equipping a person? 2 Timothy 3:16-17 says, "All Scripture is God-breathed and is useful for teaching, rebuking, correcting and training in righteousness, so that the man of God may be thoroughly equipped for every good work." Certainly every good work includes evangelism. How then do we prepare our people to share their faith? We must teach them the gospel message because it is the Scriptures themselves which make a man adequate unto every good work, including evangelism. A vast majority of believers probably know it, but they probably do not understand it well enough to effectively communicate it in a witnessing situation or other hostile environment.

The gospel is a simple truth but profound as well. Christians need to intentionally study it more. It could revolutionize our churches to truly understand the gospel, and some might get saved during the study who erroneously thought they had been saved already. Imputation, justification, propitiation, faith, grace, redemption, incarnation, and resurrection are words that go over too many Christians' heads. Yet these are essential truths that all Christians ought to know. Our Christian forefathers died for these truths. If we are able to understand them, it will be much easier to present the gospel effectively without being tied to a script. Witnessing is not automatic; it requires training and practice. If we want to see revival, we absolutely must do this step.

If pastors do not share their faith regularly and have testimonies to share accordingly, the church body will likely not share their faith either. Those who are passionate about evangelism in the congregation will probably get stifled or leave. There is a time to put down the concordance and commentaries and knock on a door or plan an outreach.

A good training program would include opportunities to practice witnessing with somebody who has more experience in it. This really helps people get over the anxiety issue about evangelism. They need to be gently but boldly drawn in to the joy of evangelism.

Outside of prayer, evangelism is probably the next worst thing with most churches. They don't do it, they don't train people to do it, and they have a list of excuses for why nobody is getting saved in our churches. If they do encourage some kind of evangelism, their emphasis is on methods rather than the message. Their church becomes proficient at conversing, but they are unable to transmit the truth. For revival to come, we must become active and proficient in prayer and witnessing by God's grace. Plain and simply, the lack of proper evangelism must be repented of and acknowledged for what it is: sin.

Excuses, Excuses, Excuses

People will give all kinds of excuses for why they do not evangelize. If it is an issue of fear, weakness, or lack of training, such things can be gently overcome and corrected. What a privilege it would be to come alongside and train someone to be able to evangelize! But many times refusing to witness is an issue of pride. This happens more in those who have been churched for a long time or in those who are study-o-holics. Others claim that the culture is so far perverted that the unsaved are incapable of receiving the gospel. There are many excuses for not sharing the gospel, but the bottom line is that the gospel still has power and still saves. Revival is tightly connected to Biblical evangelism, for revived Christians can't help but share their faith.

Seek That Which Was Lost

Luke 15 tells three stories about lost things. A man loses one sheep, a woman loses a coin, and a father loses a son to the ways of the world. A theme clearly emerges. God cares about the one, and the lost matter to God. There is more rejoicing in heaven over one sinner who repents than over ninety-nine righteous Christians. God has a heart for the lost, and so must we.

It seems that Christians get more worked up about being unable to find the television remote control than they do about their unsaved friend or family member. May God give us as individuals and churches a heart to want to do whatever we can to see salvation come to even just one lost person. The church of Jesus Christ can never be revived to the extent that our Lord wants it to be until we have a heart for the lost.

Section 5:

Then I Will "Hear, Forgive, and Heal Their Land…"

Chapter 12:
The Beautiful Bride

"Looking for the blessed hope and the appearing of the glory of our great God and Savior, Christ Jesus, who gave Himself for us to redeem us from every lawless deed, and to purify for Himself a people for His own possession, zealous for good deeds."
Titus 2:13-14

God promises that when we are revived, He will hear our prayers. Intimacy with God and the joy of our salvation will be made manifest. We can come to expect that we will receive from God what we have asked. All the ugliness and impurity of sin will be wiped away in the forgiveness found in Christ. God will no longer hide His face from us or turn His face against us. This is the love that Christ has for His beautiful bride, the church.

God's Healing Brings Holiness

The promise of 2 Chronicles 7:14 is that prayer will be answered, that God will forgive and no longer be withholding His blessing, and that what was damaged will be healed. In context, what was damaged was the literal land by locust, plague, and other adverse events, which were part of the curse should Israel not obey. God promised Israel that, if they would repent, He would restore the land to productivity and newness. In a similar vein, in New Testament times we can expect God to help the church regain its fruitfulness and holiness. God is all about healing the devastating, ravaging effects of sin. Where sin has done its dirty work and where relationships, minds, and hearts have been damaged, God can do a renewing work. Where the church has become an ugly spectacle in society because of its own hypocrisy and liberalism, it can become a beacon of light that brings conviction and hope. As Ephesians 5:26-27 says regarding Christ and His church, "so that He might sanctify her, having cleansed her by the washing of water with the word, that He might present to Himself the church in all her glory, having no spot or wrinkle or any such thing; but that she would be holy and blameless." We know He will sanctify us completely when He takes us to heaven to be with Him. Yet the goal is that His will would be done on earth as it is in heaven. In other words, we should pray for God to do a cleansing and sanctifying work in His church that the world has yet to see. We should long to be mirror images of the purity of Christ Himself. Though perfection this side of eternity is unattainable, there should remain in our hearts a relentless desire and pursuit to be the beautiful and spotless bride of Christ.

Yet perhaps we do not want this because, if others see Christ in us, we will certainly get persecuted. 2 Timothy 3:12 says, "Indeed, all who desire to live godly in Christ Jesus will be persecuted." The question is not whether or not we will be persecuted. The answer to that is already given in the affirmative. The question at hand for us is whether or not we will live godly lives before our Lord. If only the church would live as those who have been revived, society would be impacted. Culture may not change, but it will be confronted. The church can show the world what a godly culture looks like. We definitely need healing in this way.

What Does a Godly Culture Look Like?

A godly culture looks like the early church. The world's culture will always be different from the church's culture, yet we must set the example of what culture ought to be. Acts 2:42-47 says of the early church,

> "They were continually devoting themselves to the apostles' teaching and to fellowship, to the breaking of bread and to prayer. Everyone kept feeling a sense of awe; and many wonders and signs were taking place through the apostles. And all those who had believed were together and had all things in common; and they began selling their property and possessions and were sharing them with all, as anyone might have need. Day by day continuing with one mind in the temple, and breaking bread from house to house, they were taking their meals together with

gladness and sincerity of heart, praising God and having favor with all the people. And the Lord was adding to their number day by day those who were being saved."

This is true community. It is not forced, fake, or for show. Let us consider and explore what this passage says about what made the early church so special.

The early church was devoted to learning God's Word. There was an enthusiasm to continually take in as much teaching about God's Word as possible. In our day, we get angry if the message goes on for more than forty minutes. The early Christians, however, were devoting themselves to the apostles teaching continually. They took in as much as they could get. Of course, it helps that they actually had sound teachers that they could learn from. This is not to say that the believers stopped working just so that they could go to church all the time. Rather, it is that insomuch as they were able, they took advantage of every opportunity to hear the Word preached and to learn. It wasn't because it was forced upon them or a legalistic expectation. Their love for God and their desire to know Him more was so powerful that they couldn't help themselves from discussing God's Word, from sharing what they were learning with others, and from seeking wisdom from those who clearly were being led of God. Too often in modern Christianity we do not want to learn. Learning is difficult, requiring effort, attention, and concentration. Theology, after all, is the study of God. However, God is not boring, and He is the ultimate in relevance. If a sermon makes God boring or if we as a people have developed ears to hear only what we want to hear, that is the problem. It is not God or His Word that is to blame.

It ought to be that we have such an appetite for the Word of God that it is always on our thoughts and near our lips. It is what comes out of a man that defiles him, and sadly it seems that the topics of conversation in Christian circles are more frequently filled with trivial and immoral things than they are with the things of God. We must develop an attitude about the Word of God in which we approach the Scriptures as if they are our very life, food, and sustenance. We need the Word of God, each and every Word, from beginning to end. May God give us hearts to believe the entirety of Scripture and to seek to learn it from cover to cover.

The early church experienced authentic community. The early church devoted themselves to fellowship with one another and with the apostles. They needed to interact with the apostles so that they could see modeled what the apostles were teaching. The early church understood that the apostles had been with Christ and were called by God to be their shepherds and teachers. They were willing and eager to learn from these godly men and for good reason.

The apostles' ministry was more than just locking themselves away in a study for prayer and Bible reading only to make an appearance once on a Sunday. They certainly did devote themselves to prayer and study, but they also were part of the community, eating, praying, rejoicing, and praising God. An integral part of the fellowship of the early church was that they shared meals together with gladness and sincerity, praising God. It wasn't merely the after-church potluck, though that could be a decent starting point. It wasn't just the agape feast which was regularly celebrated. It was the informal, unplanned getting together of believers with one another. The western church parcels people into age groups and stages of life. The young couples go one place, but, if they have kids, then they go somewhere else. The single elderly folks are separated from the young singles as well as the married elderly. This is not the picture painted in this passage. It is the entire body, young and old, married and single, loving one another, learning from one another, and interacting with one another. This is why many commands are given in the New Testament regarding the bridging of age groups, such as that the older women teach the younger and that the younger men be in subjection to the elders. There is to be an interacting, a learning, and not a separation. This is not to say that there is never a time or place for breaking up into certain groupings, but it is to say that we need to regain an emphasis and understanding of the value of family and the benefit of learning from those in different stages of life.

We must note that the meals were taken with gladness, sincerity, and with the praising of God. The richer the individuals' relationship with Christ, the richer the fellowship could have been. It is easy to have fellowship when Christ is truly the center and not the fact that we all attend the same building on Sunday morning. We are all family in the Lord, fighting the same fight, serving the same risen Lord. This is our common bond, not that we are all members of such and such a church.

If a church body becomes focused on church itself, fellowship becomes distasteful. If the church body is focused on Christ and mission, then fellowship sweetens. Some really sweet fellowship can emerge when we serve the Lord together, laboring together in a common purpose. It doesn't happen in the thirty second period of greeting one another during the service. True fellowship is predicated upon sincerity of heart and motive, gladness, and the fact that the exaltation of God is central to the relationship and interaction.

The world can get together and small talk for hours. There are country clubs, restaurants, and sports bars for that kind of interaction. What separates the fellowship of the church from the camaraderie of the world is the fact that the centerpiece of life, interest, and conversation is the Lord. Sometimes it seems that the crowning virtue of a particular church body is that they are nice to one another. Sin and personal annoyances are tolerated for the sake of being nice. This is ugly, fake, and sickening. No one really enjoys this type of interaction, and certainly the world will want no part in it. Genuine love between believers deals with sin issues, and it is more concerned with mission and holiness than it is about being nice and small talking. Just because a few Christians gather together does not mean that some real, edifying fellowship has taken place. Fellowship in the fullest sense goes beyond just discussing the latest news and views, for, fundamentally, community is about God and not us. When we journey together in sanctification toward Christ, authentic community is possible. When we serve together and labor as one, true community will develop. When the body of Christ gathers together, we cannot afford to forget our Head.

The early church devoted themselves to praying together. Prayer as a church was likely informal, spontaneous, as well as formal and on regular occasions. Since the fellowship was God-centered, they may as well have called out to Him when they fellowshipped together. We need God to be more central in the conversations, relationships, and interactions that happen in and among our churches. Community doesn't just happen because a group of people have made a common profession to serve God. True community happens when relationships form around the centerpiece of relationship to God and the enthusiasm and active commitment to serving God. As long as sound doctrine is not compromised, even a prayer meeting causes community to develop.

One of the most caring things we can do for one another is to pray for one another. When we cast ourselves together upon the grace of God, it really is a beautiful thing.

The first Christians were described as feeling a sense of awe. In Acts, it seems that there was an excitement to assemble together, even on days besides Sunday. Their lives were consumed with Scripture, praying, studying, and fellowship. Yet they still managed to do their jobs and attend to their families. Christ permeated every area of their lives; there was no selfish compartmentalization.

No program, background music, or other artificial means can generate such awe. Picking a peppy song to begin worship with to get people "into it" is not going to create the awe. It is the work of the Spirit reviving His people to live sanctified lives and then filling them to worship and serve Him that alone can do this. Having zeal and preaching the Word is a start, but it is insufficient unless the Spirit fills and moves. Perhaps the most significant thing that we do as churches which keeps this awe-inspiring encounter away is that we don't make the service first and foremost about God. We don't approach God in fear and trembling. There is something about how we worship that is much too casual for being in the presence of a holy and all-powerful God. Awe is not merely something that we feel. It is a trembling in our spirits before the wonder and majesty of the King of Kings. It is a joy that overwhelms us because the God Who is all powerful loves us and died for us. It is all about Him. When we get consumed with God, we must necessarily be purified and overcome with an awe that He would choose to love us. There are times in Scripture where the apostle Paul spontaneously breaks out into doxology, praising God for who He is and for what He has done. Such instances of praising always follow an explanation of theology and doctrine. It is worship in spirit and in truth that draws our hearts heavenward toward God. Hearts free from outstanding sin and minds filled with the Word of God are central to encountering the awesomeness of God. How worthy He is of our praise, honor, glory, and thanksgiving! This is what we will sing when we are in heaven (Revelation 5:12). We will be utterly taken by His wonder and glory. It will have nothing to do with us, what we can do for God, or any musical rendition that we can humanly conjure up.

Our focus can get off God in many ways. This can happen when a song leader or worship team talks to the congregation and tells them to try harder, sing louder, move around more, and so on. It happens when the worship leader thanks the congregation for their singing or when he tells them that their singing was particularly good that day. It happens when we applaud after the worship team sings or after a person sings a solo. It happens when the worship leader comments about the nature of choruses and hymns, giving validity to the one or the other, rather than pointing out how the lyrics call our focus toward God. It happens when we overemphasize the experience of worship and feeling "worshipful" rather than on concentrating on the words of truth in the songs which testify to the power, majesty, and awe of God. Sadly, many contemporary songs don't draw our attention to God because they are about us. Rather than telling God we want to worship Him, that we will worship Him, or that we are hungry for Him, we ought to go ahead and actually praise Him. We sing an entire song talking about the fact that we need Him when we ought to be praising Him in light of that fact.

Another thing that detracts from the awe is breaking up services with announcements or a time of greeting that is really too short to accomplish much that is of real value anyway. This really draws our attention back to ourselves and to our schedules. We ought to try to get the announcements out of the way before the call to worship or just create an expectation that people must read the bulletin. During the Lord's Supper, if we do not regularly explain what it is for and truly take the time to remember Christ's suffering and sacrificial death, our minds will wander from the awesome encounter with God. When the pastor preaches, if he makes it too casual, often by joke-telling and story-telling for the first fifteen minutes, we will lose our focus on God. We might become enraptured in the story or in the preacher himself, but we will not be enraptured with God. We need God's Word to encounter God. Stories, jokes, gimmicks, props, and vocal inflections will not get the job done. Worship is through truth.

How the pastor approaches the Word of God also will affect our ability to see how awesome God is. If he casually references a verse here or there and then talks only on abstract things hardly related, we will likely fail to encounter God because we have journeyed outside of His Word. We begin putting more emphasis on what the pastor says and how he says it than on what the Word says and how God says it. We must approach God in reverence, awe, and fear. We are those under authority of One deserving all praise, glory, and honor. When we do anything to put the focus on ourselves, we steal His glory. May it never be, for God will have none of it.

The early Christians possessed an unusual generosity. Those who had an excess of wealth sold the excess and gave to those who had a lack. This wasn't a version of socialism where the church government set wages and standards of living. It was a cheerful giving to ensure that everybody had what they needed, within the church and without. It says they gave to all as there was need. Many today live in gross excess, groaning internally about giving to God. Some who are in need are afraid to ask the church for help because of the impending judgment and rebuke for living irresponsibly that they would likely receive. God says that the poor will always be among us. Some people have disabilities, poor health, or suffer divinely orchestrated difficulties and tragedies. Compassion is in order in such cases. Of course, there are those who do exploit the system, and church leaders must be discerning in such matters. The bottom line is that, when compared to the early church, today's church is far less generous. This leads inevitably to less unity, less love, less fellowship, and less community. When some lack while others hold back, God's family is harmed. We need to be freer with what God has given us, we need to sacrifice more as He leads us, and we need to remember that all wealth is God's wealth.

The early Christians were of one mind. Paul exhorted the Philippians in 2:2, saying, "Make my joy complete by being of the same mind, maintaining the same love, united in spirit, intent on one purpose." True community requires that we have the same mind toward one another. Romans 12:6 says, "Be of the same mind toward one another; do not be haughty in mind, but associate with the lowly. Do not be wise in your own estimation." Being of the same mind requires that we do not live according to a mindset that ranks one another or compares one another. We are not to think of ourselves as better than somebody else because of who we are, because of what we do, or because of what we have. There is no partiality with God, nor can we afford to have such partiality for the sake of fellowship and unity. We are to maintain the same love and be united in spirit, otherwise divisions and factions will emerge as they did at Corinth. Some thought they were of Paul, and some claimed allegiance to Apollos. The reality is that we are all Christ's, and He is the unifying factor. 1 Corinthians 1:10 says, "Now I exhort you, brethren, by the name of our Lord Jesus Christ, that you all agree and that there be no divisions among you, but that you be made complete in the same mind and in the same judgment." Today's church is full of divisions, and the only hope of unity is through humility, doctrinal purity, and being of the same mind. Only the grace of God can move us in the right direction. As we pray for revival, we must seek true unity, in doctrine and in life.

The early community of faith had the favor of those outside of the church. Certainly this was not true of all outside the church. The religious leaders and Pharisees wanted to squelch the movement, but many other Jews and Gentiles were interested because of the testimony of joy and purity of the early church. Where else did people sell property to give to those in need? Where else did people go out of their way to care for the sick and forgotten lying on the street corner? When something exciting and awesome is taking place within a community of faith, even those outside of the church take notice. The assertion by many in the world today is that church is boring and irrelevant. We in our fleshly ways have tried to energize the presentation and dramatize the communication so as to draw in more carnal people by carnal means. We need to have an environment like the early church which had this God-generated awe without any of the manmade bells and whistles. It is God who energizes and gives the power. Every church leader ought to be praying that God would develop a similar sense of awe in their local body of believers. They ought also to be praying for holiness in their churches because there can be no infusion of the power of God or the filling of the Spirit without clean vessels. The watching world noticed something different, special, and unique that only God could have done. Even those who hated the Christians couldn't condemn them on the basis of their character and integrity. Their testimony was too strong, too wide, and too pure. The early church had favor because of their testimony. May it be the same in our day and in our churches.

Finally, the early church received a blessing of conversions. We learn that the Lord added daily to their number those who were being saved. It wasn't that the church was cloistered in some room tucked away from the world and from reality, and God miraculously led people to them to be saved. Some Christians believe that if we are just faithful, then God will add to our number. We must be faithful, and part of faithfulness is that we share our faith and engage in personal evangelism. The early church was known for both its kindness and for sharing the gospel at every opportunity possible. There was hardly a conversation that went by without the gospel being presented. It was central to their lives, it was their identity, and they showcased it for all who were watching. We are responsible for evangelizing. God may not add to our number in the incredible way that He did in the early days of the church, but the idea is that there ought to be an adding taking place somehow, sometime, and someway. If the church is revived, effective evangelism can and should follow.

It Could Happen Again

The community pictured in Acts 2 is not something that happened once and cannot happen again. Sure, times are different, and the apostles are no longer among us. However, true fellowship and community like they experienced can happen again. Often times church is not a beautiful thing or place. Families are in disarray and conflict, and sin is allowed to go unchecked in the body. Yet Christ wants to beautify His bride, the church of Jesus Christ. The work of revival will be to make the church glow in beauty and splendor as it once did.

There is absolutely no question that the church is spiritually sick. Marriages are out of balance, children are rebellious, discipleship is poor, few witness, there is little prayer, preaching is not rooted in Scripture or by the power of God, and many live mired in sin. Yet we dare not gloat in our sickness as if it is a sign of being humble, but we must seek God's healing and restoration. The church in Acts 2 was not described by the Holy Spirit as sick in any way. Two of the churches in Revelation passed God's examination for church health and purity. A healthy church, according to God's Word, is possible and expected. In no way is it acceptable before God Who has given us all things pertaining to life and godliness for us to conclude that there is nothing that can be done to help the church heal and grow. This complacency and sub-par attitude of faithlessness must be abandoned if revival is to come. Scripture presents the possibility of the bride of Christ being beautiful, not sick and decrepit. To tolerate any lesser expectation is sin and nothing short of an utter lack of faith. Faithlessness is a blasphemy of the intention, character, and power of God. We need to be healed, and we need to be forgiven. Our testimony must be restored, and increasing fruit must be born.

God doesn't tolerate hypocrisy. If we are hypocrites, we had better repent. Otherwise, how will the world recognize us, how will they see Christ, and how will they know that God indeed sent the Son? **If God cannot change our lives by the power of Christ, why would an unbeliever suspect that He could change his?** If our church is sick, we need to be part of the healing work of God. If we do not repent, we can expect God to remove our lampstand. This is why we need revival and why the church must change.

May the Holy Spirit begin to move to show every man, woman, and child who names the name of Christ what Christ is really like and what His Word truly demands of us. May God heal His church and beautify His bride. *Revive us, Lord, according to Your lovingkindness and according to Your Word.*

www.ingramcontent.com/pod-product-compliance
Lightning Source LLC
Chambersburg PA
CBHW061441040426
42450CB00007B/1158